The United Pilot's
Flight Plan
for
WEALTH

The United Pilot's Flight Plan for Wealth

Efficient Wealth Management • 8505 Technology Forest Place • Suite 104 • The Woodlands, TX 77381

Phone: (281) 528-1200

Paul@EfficientWealthManagement.com • www.EfficientWealthManagement.com

CONTENTS

INTRODUCTION
MY STORY

I AM PASSIONATE ABOUT HELPING PEOPLE achieve the high quality of life they want for themselves and their families. My own journey has taught me how anyone can build a hugely successful and satisfying life if they work hard, make smart choices, and stay focused on their most important dreams and goals.

I was born in Dublin, Ireland. When I was very young, my family moved to London, England. Not long thereafter, my parents divorced and my mother, originally from Ireland, was left to fend for herself and three young children in a foreign country, with no legal rights to child support or otherwise. My father, from Dallas, Texas, returned to the United States.

After a number of years and extraordinary trials, my mother remarried and we moved to Manchester, England, with her new husband. Manchester is an interesting city; it is the birthplace of the Industrial Revolution. However, by the 1970s, the Industrial Revolution had moved on to more favorable business climates. The north of England was hit by a series of debilitating strikes by coal miners and others. The Labour Party had effectively dismantled any incentive to revitalize the area's economy. Youth unemployment exceeded 25 percent. My stepfather, a professional, spent a number of years during this period driving a taxi to make ends meet.

Manchester was a cold, wet, depressing city that offered nothing to a young Irishman: no job, no future and no hope. And for this I am eternally grateful. It burned into my psyche a desire to make something of myself.

Already motivated, I got direction during the summer of 1977. I was 15 years old, and my grandfather, whom I barely knew, invited me and my brother to visit him in Dallas, Texas. Despite the ongoing stagflation that had the United States in its grip, to my eyes the streets of Dallas were paved in gold. Sunshine, opportunity and hope prevailed.

My grandfather, a stockbroker at a regional firm, was larger than life. He was a highly respected, honorable, old-school advisor who was doing well for himself by taking care of others and doing well by them.

I spent the next two years figuring out how I was going to return to this land of opportunity. The one valuable legacy my now-absent father had left me was a U.S. passport. I visited the local library in Manchester and found an old Peterson's college guide. I wrote a *lot* of letters to schools. Oklahoma State University accepted me provisionally, offering me a grant for tuition and a work scholarship for room and board. There would be no money left over. But I took it.

In 1979, I left Manchester and came to the United States with nothing more than $200 and a toothbrush. I was just 17 years old when I got off that bright orange Braniff jumbo jet in Dallas—and I had no idea what I was doing. I'll never forget being at the Dallas Greyhound station, thinking to myself, "Maybe I didn't think this all through."

After three semesters at OSU, I was truly out of airspeed, altitude and ideas. The finances just didn't add up. So I decided to enlist in the U.S. Air Force as a way to continue my education.

While working full-time as an aircraft electrician, I also went to school full-time, taking night classes at the University of Maryland. I didn't sleep much in those days. Young people can get away with that. Every extra penny that I earned went to tuition and books. The military education benefits were not so good during that period: The old G.I. Bill had recently expired, and it would be about five years before it was put in place.

But I was motivated. The military was a means to an end: I wanted a degree and then I wanted to move on. As I approached the end of my tour in the military, I graduated *summa cum laude* from Maryland with a 4.0 GPA.

Both of my college experiences were great, but I still felt very new to America and didn't know what my next move should be. So I did what a lot of college graduates in that situation do: I decided to go to graduate school.

My timing was fortuitous. Texas A&M was building a world-class business school, and I was actively recruited into its graduate finance program, thanks to my good grades and high GMAT scores. Texas A&M offered quite a package: food, housing and a job—all the things a person without much support needs in order to get through college.

LIFE LESSONS LEARNED

Through-out these years, I learned a valuable lesson. Though I'd always wanted to go to the University of Texas at Austin—my father's and grandfather's alma mater—UT was not very supportive beyond accepting me into its graduate program. I made a strategic decision: Go where it's clear you're wanted.

In many ways I felt that I'd finally made it. The experiences of my youth had given me a burning desire to understand finance. I wanted to help people chart a financial course through life and to succeed while doing so.

The A&M Masters in Finance program was challenging, but I did very well. It had been almost eight years since I'd stepped off that Braniff flight in the fall of 1979. I was ready to take on the world!

However, the world had other plans for me.

I graduated into a horrendous recession in Texas that was caused by a collapse in oil prices in the 1980s. Houston's economy hit bottom in January 1987. The region had 220,000 fewer jobs than it had five years earlier.

What's more, the country was about to experience Black Monday—October 19, 1987—when stock markets around the world crashed. The Dow Jones Industrial Average shed almost 23 percent in a single day!

Texas A&M really pulled through for me. The university's Association of Former Students let me know they would do what they could to help me find a good job. They introduced me to partners at what would become Accenture Consulting. These partners flew me to the then-booming Los Angeles office and offered me a job on the spot.

Though slightly off-track, I was very fortunate to be gainfully employed by a great company.

The economy continued to recover, and I went to work at a brokerage firm called Smith Barney as I sought to get back on my preferred career track. I was sent through the firm's rigorous training program. (If you've ever seen the movie *The Pursuit of Happyness* with Will Smith, you will know what I'm talking about.) I did extremely well, scoring a rare 95 percent on the Series 7 exam the first time through.

Finally! I was excited to start helping investors make smart decisions about their money. Unfortunately, Smith Barney had other plans.

My reward for my success in graduate school and in the Smith Barney training program was a phone, a phone book and a long list of products that I was supposed to sell. They called that "dialing for dollars," and it really was not what I had in mind.

I didn't want to be cold-calling my way to success. I had learned a great deal about theories of finance and had developed a passion for taking care of people and for solving their financial problems. Cold-calling and selling airplane partnerships were not part of the deal. I wanted to put all my knowledge into action.

WHEN LIFE ALTERS YOUR FLIGHT PLAN

After a while, I realized that the financial services industry was just not set up to allow someone like me to help people the way I truly wanted to help them. At the same time, my best friend from the Air Force had been taking flying lessons and introduced me to flying. After being caught in bad weather in western Kansas, I got my instrument ticket. I was hooked.

Disillusioned, I quit Smith Barney to become a jet pilot. But then my best-laid plans were torn asunder once again by the convulsions within the airline industry. Even so, with persistence—and after seven other lousy flying jobs—I was finally hired at Continental Airlines. In due course I would become a B737 captain. Unfortunately, the worst of the industry's storm systems had yet to sweep through.

September 11, 2001, was both a terrible day for America and a devastating blow for the airline industry. Soon after that terrible day I received a furlough letter from Continental. That letter changed my life. I did some soul searching as I thought about what my next step in life would be—perhaps creating or buying a business, I thought.

Going back into the world of financial services was definitely *not* on my list. The unpleasant memories of Smith Barney's sales culture were still fresh in my mind. Then one day, a good friend of mine asked me a question:

"Why not help people with their finances *on your own terms?*"

That was just the spark I needed. I decided that I would make a difference in people's lives by building a professional wealth management practice—not one that was sales-oriented, but a client-centric one that was built along the lines of a law firm or CPA firm. I envisioned a firm that would always put my clients' interests first.

And so I created a consultative business model that included working with a team of experts to help my clients protect their wealth, mitigate their taxes, take care of their heirs, protect their assets from being unjustly taken and maximize the impact of their charitable giving. I started my firm, Efficient Wealth Management, in one room of my house, in 2003.

Today, we have a beautiful office in The Woodlands, Texas that consists of me and a talented team of professionals. We've been successful beyond my wildest imagination. Every day I get to come to work, talk to people who have become my friends, mentor them, and add value to their lives by doing what is best for them and by acting with integrity on their behalf.

I can't imagine a more rewarding career. I'm extremely fortunate that my firm's success has enabled me to focus on clients for whom I am best-suited—including airline pilots and senior executives in the airline industry. In fact, some of my closest and most loyal friends are aviators who have become clients.

WHY I WROTE THIS BOOK

I absolutely love helping people improve the quality of their lives. That is why I wrote this book—to share my passion and to give airline pilots and executives a process for making the smartest decisions about their wealth. I hope you enjoy reading this book and find within it the tools you need to achieve all that is truly important to you and to the people in your life whom you care about most.

CHAPTER ONE

SETTING THE RIGHT COURSE

AS A LEADING MEMBER OF THE AIRLINE INDUSTRY, you have the potential to do extremely well financially for yourself, your family and others you care about most. That said, I can't emphasize enough that you also face tremendous challenges in your journey to a secure, comfortable and meaningful financial future.

This book is written with you in mind. Its entire purpose is to help you in your efforts as a highly compensated airline industry professional position your wealth so that you can achieve all that is truly most important to you.

In many ways, you are like the majority of affluent professionals who wonder whether they are making intelligent decisions about their wealth. Like them, you might feel uncertain about your investment strategy. You might get nervous when you read headlines that predict a bleak day (or month or year) for the financial markets. And you might chase after hot investments that you hear about from friends and colleagues—"sure thing" winners that you can't bear to pass up, lest you watch your peers strike it rich or retire years before you do.

But in other ways, you face unique issues due to your chosen career. Airline industry professionals must contend with a stormy sky full of turbulence—from changing global economic conditions and pilot contracts to a confusing array of benefits plans and uncertainty about the future of the airlines themselves.

When you think about all the airline-specific challenges you face coupled with the myriad general concerns that you share with the rest of the affluent community, it's no surprise that many of you desire a better way to build a stable and strong financial future for yourselves.

A FRAMEWORK FOR INTELLIGENT FINANCIAL DECISION MAKING

What you need is exactly what is presented in the pages that follow: a framework for understanding how the markets truly operate, so that you can position your assets to work with those markets—not against them—and achieve a level of success you may not have thought possible.

This framework is built on a foundation of several key tenets of intelligent investing, such as:

- Take only investment risks for which you're fairly compensated.
- Leverage the power of diversification to increase returns and reduce volatility.
- Build asset class portfolios that capture each market's inherent rate of return.
- Monitor your progress to stay disciplined and committed to your plan.

This book will explore each of these key tenets in great detail so you understand not just the basics of each one, but also how to implement each one as part of a successful, holistic investment portfolio strategy.

As you will see, this framework is rooted in deep academic research conducted by some of the sharpest minds in the investment universe. These experts, and the ground breaking research they have conducted, have shown us a path to success based on what works in the real world. By implementing these proven techniques, you will position yourself for maximum success. What's more, you will enjoy a greater sense of security and the peace of mind that comes with the knowledge and confidence that you are taking the right steps to achieve a comfortable future.

The vast majority of investors are not aware of most (if not all) of these key tenets of successful investing—even though they have been rigorously tested and shown to work. The reason is that much of the advice that investors get comes from big Wall Street firms and other financial services behemoths that take a fundamentally different approach to investing than we do.

These firms will tell you that their approach is far superior to the one in this book. Unfortunately—for them—the numbers and facts in this book confirm a very different story. If the approach detailed in this book was more widely known and used by investors, it would damage the fortunes of the large financial services companies. More investors would come to realize that the "advice" they've been getting for so long from the broker-dealers and wirehouses was meant to serve the best interests of the investment firms—not the investors.

A COORDINATED APPROACH TO MANAGING WEALTH COMPREHENSIVELY

All that said, a framework for investing is only part (albeit a large part) of the solution you need. The benefits of intelligent investing can be truly maximized only when they are part of a larger whole—a comprehensive and coordinated plan for managing not just investments but also your entire financial situation.

This coordinated plan is what I call wealth management. It is a process for making sure that all the "moving parts" of your financial life work in concert with each other. From investing to tax strategies to retirement planning to asset protection and charitable giving, wealth management is designed to provide integrated solutions to the biggest challenges and opportunities you face as a successful airline professional.

Wealth management is characterized by three main components:

1. **Investment consulting**—strategies for growing and protecting wealth by positioning investment capital in optimal ways.

2. **Advanced planning**—strategies for addressing non-investment goals (including asset protection and estate planning) that play important roles in the lives of affluent investors.

3. **Relationship management**—strategies for helping clients create investment and advanced planning solutions in partnership with a team of dedicated financial professionals who are managed by a personal Chief Financial Officer (CFO), your Wealth Manager.

What's more, wealth management is delivered using a well-defined process involving a series of formal meetings between investor and advisor. These meetings, outlined in chapter 11, are designed to establish a highly collaborative relationship between advisors and their clients.

The upshot: By the time you finish this book, you will understand how to invest better than the vast majority of investors out there today. And you will understand the right process for managing *all* of your wealth intelligently. At that point, you truly will have a flight plan for wealth that will enable you to reach your destination on time and in comfort.

But to get there, you have to be realistic about the challenges you'll encounter along the way. In the next chapter, we'll explore the key issues you face as an airline executive and the implications they are likely to have on your financial future. Armed with that information and with a sense of clarity, you can begin to formulate the right plan for achieving your goals.

CHAPTER 2
ISSUES FACING PILOTS TODAY—AND GOING FORWARD

ECONOMIC AND FISCAL CHALLENGES, both in the U.S. and abroad, have reshaped the airline industry and created uncertainty for pilots, including those working for major airlines. The industry landscape has fundamentally changed. The stresses of the past decade have forced substantial consolidation, forcing an overdue rationalization of the business.

The Continental/United merger of 2010, along with vexing regulatory changes, has added a great deal of complexity and uncertainty to pilots' retirement and benefits options.

In this environment, pilots face challenges in two major categories: External and internal.

1. **External challenges** include the global economy, the state of the airlines, the Continental/United merger, and related uncertainty about the latest pilot contract signed in 2013, and complex benefit plans. These external challenges are akin to bad weather: you can plan for the possibilities, you can see them coming and you can alter your route accordingly, but there's no avoiding some level of turbulence.

2. Internal challenges are behavioral issues that pilots may control. These issues include inadequate saving, excessive spending, unstructured financial planning, and lack of financial education, among others. These internal challenges are akin to unusual flight attitudes: Once pilots are made aware of them, they can take steps to adjust and regain control.

The challenges above can be addressed, even eliminated, with a disciplined approach to wealth management. With the right process and "crew" in place, you will be equipped to regain control over your internal behavioral challenges, and even better equipped to handle the ups and downs of external industry challenges.

THE KEY RETIREMENT ISSUES FACED BY SENIOR AIRLINE PILOTS

Our firm surveyed senior airline pilots about their most pressing retirement-related financial concerns. As seen in Figure 2.1, they identified a wide range of issues. The most pressing concerns included protecting wealth, planning for retirement and maintaining their current lifestyle in retirement.

Figure 2.1: Pilots' Retirement Planning Priorities

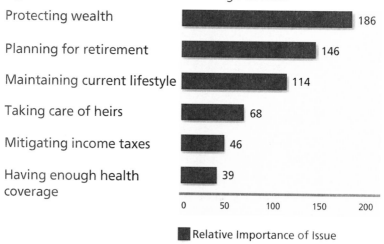

Source: Efficient Wealth Management survey of senior airline pilots, 2010.

Figure 2.2: Pilot Satisfaction with Current Retirement Preparation

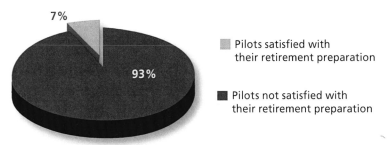

7%

93%

■ Pilots satisfied with their retirement preparation

■ Pilots not satisfied with their retirement preparation

Source: Efficient Wealth Management survey of senior airline pilots, 2010.

The vast majority of senior pilots do not feel satisfied with their retirement preparation thus far. Our research revealed that 93 percent of pilots did not feel they had been successful in addressing their financial challenges (see Figure 2.2).

Clearly there is a great need for more effective retirement planning within the pilot community, and there's a relatively broad definition of what retirement planning entails for pilots. That definition is far broader than one describing a traditional approach to investment management.

Pilots are increasingly required to take over the controls when it comes to their own retirement planning. A survey[1] by one wealth management firm indicated that while airlines used to contribute a portion of pilots' salary to defined benefit plans managed by professional advisors, pilots are now largely responsible for their own retirement via contributions to 401(k) plans. The survey found that 80 percent of pilots contributed to their retirement plans. About two in five pilots (41 percent) contributed between 11 percent and 20 percent of their incomes to retirement plans, and one in eight pilots (12 percent) contribute more than 20 percent of their incomes to retirement plans.

What's more, three out of five pilots (60 percent) used the 401(k) Personal Choice Retirement Account (PCRA), a brokerage window that allows them to invest in individual stocks, bonds and mutual funds that are not included in their plan's core investment lineup.

As the burden for retirement planning shifts to pilots themselves, they face a dilemma. Pilots recognize the need to take action and ownership over their planning. But many pilots also fear that they lack the time, knowledge, expertise or confidence needed to manage their own wealth effectively. For these pilots, professional financial advice is becoming a priority. For example, the aforementioned survey found that nearly one fourth of pilots (24 percent) already worked with an investment advisor. Nearly two-thirds (63 percent) said they **would want to work with** an advisor to help them meet their retirement goals.

EXTERNAL FACTORS AFFECTING PILOTS' FINANCIAL AND RETIREMENT SECURITY

Weakness in both the economy and the airline industry has made many pilots justifiably concerned about their financial futures. Just as turbulence can come unexpectedly and make for an uncomfortable flight, recent economic and industry events have changed the financial comfort level of many pilots.

The airline industry has endured unprecedented stress in the past 15 years and airline prosperity is no longer guaranteed. Downward pressure on fare prices combined with rising fuel costs has squeezed margins on both sides of the balance sheet. These and other pressures have driven airlines to reduce other costs, including labor, in an effort to remain profitable. Take-home pay has decreased, in some cases by as much as 30- to 40-percent[2] according to a 2010 *USA Today* article. As a result, employment levels have dropped, pilots have been furloughed, and defined-benefit pension plans have been eliminated or frozen. The recent merger of Continental and United raises uncertainty about the retirement options that will be available for the combined company's pilot group, as the Continental pension plan was significantly different from United's. Meanwhile the huge wave of pilots approaching retirement age could create renewed pressure on the retirement plans' funding.

1. Recession. **Between 1995 and 2001, revenue passenger miles rose 28.1 percent and employment expanded by nearly 20 percent. This unprecedented growth and expansion left the airline industry unprepared for 9/11 and the economic downturn that followed. While employment levels reached record levels in March 2001, they declined in each of the following five years, according to a 2008 *Monthly Labor Review* report.[3]**

This permanently changed the financial picture for many pilots, and has certainly changed the comfortable assumption of lifetime employment industry wide. It is imperative that each pilot, no matter where they may be in their career, "takes the helm" of their own retirement planning and strongly consider the exposure to career risks that include unemployment, furlough or salary reduction.

Figure 2.3 illustrates the impact on Continental and United pilots. As of 2009, Continental had shed 9 percent of its pilot workforce while United lost 43 percent, representing a total loss of more than 4,500 jobs among those two airlines alone.

Figure 2.3: Percentage Change in Pilot Jobs 2000-2010

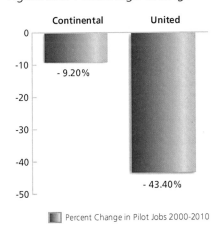

Source: Airline Financials.com; Airline Analysis; June 2011

2. Industry consolidation and recovery. When we put together our white paper back in 2010, the airline industry was coming out of one of its darkest periods ever—the combination of 9/11 and the subsequent recession. Then we saw the beginnings of a recovery only to be thwarted by the financial collapse of 2008. These events resulted in an industry that frankly had to consolidate. It's no great surprise that consolidation was predicted. The reality is that consolidation—effective consolidation—didn't happen until it was forced by the sheer survival needs of the industry.

Pilot salaries will likely never return to the lofty levels of the 1970s (adjusted for inflation). On the other hand, they're unlikely to drop to where they were in the late '80s and '90s and 2000s either. The worst is definitely over for pilots, but the increased costs imposed both by the recovery of pilot salaries and the new rest rules (FAR 117) will create additional incentive for the airlines to find a more efficient way to man their aircraft.

3. Industry demographics. A shortage of qualified pilots has hit U.S. airlines sooner and more severely than expected, forcing the airlines to accelerate hiring and cut some services.

According to a February 2014 *Wall Street Journal* story,[4] United CEO, Jeff Smisek said in an employee memo that regional airline partners "are beginning to have difficulty flying their schedules due to reduced new-pilot availability and plan to reduce [regional airline] flying in our most unprofitable markets."

The shortage flows from both a long anticipated wave of pilot retirements, and recently enacted rules that require an increase in training for new pilots and more rest for existing aviators at airlines. The rate of loss was slowed by the raising of the retiring age in 2007. Many pilots started their careers in the 1980s and the demographic bump is approaching the mandatory retirement age of 65 rapidly. Moreover, though this age limit may be changed at some point, the relief to the airlines will be modest and fleeting.

Figure 2.4: Emptying Seats

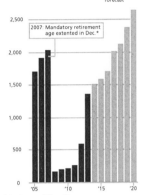

Emptying Seats
Number of pilots retiring from major U.S. airlnes

forecast

2007: Mandatory retirement age extented in Dec.*

*Extended to 65 years old from 60
Note: Includes carriers that fly large jets with more than $1 billion annual revenue
Source: KitDarby.com Aviation Consulting, *The Wall Street Journal*

Source: Kit Darby. Kitdarby.com. Atlanta, GA

At some point, the technology, staffing and financial pressures will intersect to compel the industry to move to single pilot operations supplemented by ground station based support pilots. This will be fought, tooth and nail, by the unions and other groups, but the economics are compelling, as was noted in a recent article in The *Economist*[5] These pressures imply substantial career risk for the youngest, most junior pilots, once this transition begins.

4. Changing retirement plan options. With the future of the industry hazy, the outlook for pilots' retirement plans is also unclear. At the time of this writing, Legacy Continental Airlines pilots' defined-benefit pension plan is frozen, accruing no additional benefits. Legacy United Airlines cancelled its pension during the company's last bankruptcy, and their pilots have seen benefits reduced, in some cases by as much as 70 percent, under the government's Pension Benefit Guarantee Corps' (PBGC) oversight of the plan.[6]

The PBGC does not provide lump sum payouts, except when the total benefit is under $5,000. Furthermore, the PBGC's maximum monthly guarantees for people age 65 and over are capped at

$4,943.18 for Straight-Life Annuity in 2014 and $4,448.86 if you have a joint and 50 percent survivor annuity.[7] If the annuity is taken at 60, the maximum monthly benefit for Straight-Life is $3,213.07 and only $2,891.76 for Joint and 50 Percent Survivor Annuity.

Under Legacy Continental's existing defined-benefit pension plan, Legacy Continental pilots can qualify for as much as $900,000 in a lump sum upon retirement.[8] While it is highly unlikely that Legacy Continental's pension would be turned over to the PBGC any time soon, it is possible that, if funding is depleted, pilots would be forced to annuitize their benefits.

However, the new pilot contract at United has vastly improved the pay and benefits of pilots from both legacy Continental and legacy United Airlines.

In this environment, it is imperative to re-examine your goals and plans. Be sure they are realistic and take into account all of the realities of the present environment. Even if you are nearing retirement, your financial security is not a foregone conclusion. But no matter where you are in your career, the best way to maximize your financial results is to adopt an appropriate planning approach as early as possible. Even in today's environment, with proper planning, it remains possible to build a robust "flight plan" for retirement that will improve the probability that you will enjoy the post-work lifestyle you envision, regardless of environmental factors.

THE PILOT PERSONALITY—INTERNAL AND BEHAVIORAL FACTORS AFFECTING PILOTS' FINANCIAL AND RETIREMENT SECURITY

Compounding the negative impact of industry events, many pilots' retirement goals have been compromised by their own behaviors.[9] Our firm's 2010 survey of senior airline pilots posed questions about retirement-readiness and pilots' barriers to financial success. Almost universally, the pilots interviewed expressed a high degree of concern about their level of preparation for retirement.

Behavioral finance gives us tools to understand better the behavioral challenges interfering with pilots' retirement preparation. Behavioral finance uses social, cognitive and emotional factors in understanding the economic decisions of individuals. Daniel Kahneman, who received the 2002 Nobel Prize in Economics for "integrating insights from psychological research into economic science,"[10] gives us some clues. The focus of this field of study is to understand how factors that result in mental heuristics, or shortcuts, may cause otherwise intelligent pilots to engage repetitively in flawed logic that results in poor financial decisions.

Some of the more frequently encountered mental shortcuts include using rules of thumb, not strict logic, for decision making. Other shortcuts are more emotionally biased, such as loss aversion (the strong preference to avoid losses over equivalent gains), and overconfidence—overestimating one's ability to save and invest successfully and prudently. As most airline pilots are highly confident individuals, there's a tendency to exhibit a strong "overconfidence bias" when it comes to financial matters.

Another mental shortcut commonly found among pilots is the tendency to think in nominal terms, rather than in real terms. Nominal accounting does not account for the impact of inflation. This results in what's known as "Money Illusion," in which an investor disregards the extent to which inflation cuts into the future purchasing power of pay scales and investments.

These are just a few of the many behavioral factors that affect the financial decision making of pilots (and most other adults for that matter). During our interviews, we discovered three common behavioral challenges:

1. Insufficient savings during the early years of one's career. A common behavioral error is to be overconfident about ones' ability to save and invest in future years. As a result, inadequate savings in early years causes investors to miss out on the benefits of compound interest—the most powerful force in an investment portfolio. This error has been exacerbated among the pilot community, which had long assumed that a defined-benefit (fixed) pension and other retirement benefits would be forthcoming to them. Consequently, many pilots have surprisingly inadequate savings as they approach mandatory retirement age.

2. Uncertainty resulting from adverse market conditions. Other pilots have saved fairly aggressively, but have seen their savings shredded by a series of severe bear markets coupled with their predictable response to sell once reaching their threshold of pain. Unfortunately, loss aversion and pilots' herd-like return to markets *after* they've recovered is what causes them to keep making the classic mistake of buying high and selling low. All too often, frustrated pilots conclude that the investment "game" is somehow rigged against them and they revert to "stable" assets that are, historically, unable to keep up with the demands of inflation and taxes.

3. Insufficient time and resources to become skilled investment practitioners. There is no reason why a pilot who has the spatial intelligence to fly a jet cannot manage his or her own portfolio successfully. However, significant hurdles that are not always apparent to the aviator confront the would-be-investor. Pilots are used to having highly structured and well-defined training programs. These programs guide the neophyte in a very deliberate, time-tested manner—from his first walk-around inspection through flying solo, to the leadership and technical skills demanded of the captain of a sophisticated jet. And no amount of training can make up for lack of experience.

This is also true of finance. But, while there's not much disagreement about how to fly a jet, there's a lot of disagreement about how to invest successfully. This conundrum became quite clear in our survey of pilots as they frequently mentioned both the lack of time (alongside a general disinterest in allocating their time to investment matters), and the difficulty of identifying and utilizing resources needed to learn the skills required to invest and grow a portfolio for retirement.

For pilots who want to do their own investing, The Certified Financial Planner™ (CFP®) credential is a graduate-level accrediting program that links theory and practice in financial markets and retirement planning. It provides the groundwork to enable any investor to make smart decisions about whether or not they would like to self-manage their portfolio. The CFP® also provides guidance about how to proceed in the development of one's financial knowledge and experience. Without experience, however, this credential is akin to having an ATP with little or no flight hours, The CFP® stands out as a "must-have" credential for any serious professional advisor that you're evaluating.

THERE IS NO TIME TO WASTE

Until recently, being a pilot was viewed as a profession that provided prestige, financial stability and the prospect of a comfortable retirement. Today the profession is rife with uncertainty. It's no wonder that pilots told us in our comprehensive 2010 survey that they are not well prepared for retirement.

It is clear that the airline industry is far too volatile, and that pension benefits are far too uncertain, for any senior pilot to take a "wait and see" attitude with regard to retirement. What's more, there are internal factors—behavioral tendencies—that seek to work against our ability to make smart financial decisions. Given all of these challenges, it is time to create your own "flight plan" for retirement, so that no matter the weather, you will have adequate fuel for the destination of your choice.

1 Cleary Gull, "Survey of Airline Pilots Find Most Are Engaged Retirement Investors" Jan. 21, 2014

2 Jones, Charisse. "Add 'Pilot' to List of Jobs That Aren't So Great Now," *USA Today* Feb. 22, 2010

3 Goodman, Christopher. "Takeoff and Descent of Airline Employment." *Monthly Labor Review.* October 2008: 5,11.

4 Carey, Susan and Nicas, Jack. "Airline Pilot Shortage Arrives Ahead of Schedule." *Wall Street Journal.* Feb. 3, 2014.

5 "A Mighty Contest: Job Destruction by Robots Could Outweigh Creation." *The Economist.* March, 29, 2014.

6 Ruskoff, Dale. "Human Toll of a Pension Default." *The Washington Post.* June 6, 2013

7 http://www.pbgc.gov/about/faq/pg/general-faqs-about-pbgc.html. *PBCG.* April 26, 2011

8 Glenn Brown & Besty Brown v. Continental Airlines. Case 4:09-cv-01148 Document 23. United States District Court Southern District of Texas Houston Division. October 2009. Print

9 Efficient Wealth Management Pilots Survey 2010

10 Nobel Prizes 2002, Nobelprize.org Aug. 2, 2011 http://nobelprize.org/nobel_prize/lists

CHAPTER THREE

THE NEW UNITED AIRLINES: COMPLEX BENEFITS IN A COMPLEX INDUSTRY

THE TERMINATION AND FREEZE of the two legacy carriers' (United and Continental) classic Defined Benefit (DB) pension plans, coupled with the long-awaited improved negotiating position of the pilot groups, have created an impetus for new and vastly more complex benefits for most airline pilots, particularly the new United's.

In this chapter, we will summarize the important benefits available to you, a United pilot, with our analysis and recommendations about the most valuable strategies you can deploy given these benefits. We'll also discuss the truth of the heavily sold "guaranteed annuity" products and, for those who would prefer a true guarantee at any cost, we'll discuss a cheaper, safer solution that also enjoys a market upside along with true longevity protection.

FOUR TYPES OF BENEFITS

Broadly speaking, your benefits fall into one of four categories:

Cat. I: **Classic Pensions**, formally known as Defined Benefit (DB) plans or the "A-Plan."

Cat. II: Defined Contribution plans, recognized as the 401(k), the "B-Plan" and "C-Plan" (legacy UAL only), and the "SERP" (Supplemental Employee Retirement Plan) for senior management pilots.

Cat. III: New hybrid insurance savings plans, such as the VEBA RHA, the HSA, FSA, and the MetLife VUL insurance products.

Cat. IV: More traditional benefits along with attractive new retiree medical benefits for the pilots.

Cat. I: Classic Pensions, or Defined Benefit plans

These are employer-sponsored retirement plans in which employee benefits are sorted out based on a formula using such factors as salary history and duration of employment. Under this type of plan, investment risk and portfolio management are entirely under the company's control—not yours.

A Defined Benefit plan is different from a Defined Contribution plan in which Defined Benefit payouts are dependent on the return achieved by the invested funds and contributions. Consequently, United is required to increase scheduled contributions whenever returns from investments devoted to funding the employee's retirement plan and paying benefits to fellow pilots result in a funding shortfall.

For purposes of this discussion, there were three relevant pensions at the legacy carriers that make up the "new United" as we know it today. Legacy Continental brought two main pension plans to the new United:

1. Continental Pilots Retirement Plan, or CPRP.

2. Continental Airlines Retirement Plan, or CARP, was originally for all eligible employees of the airline. This benefit program ended for most pilots when CPRP was carved out and frozen as part of contract concessions that were signed during the severe airline recession that

followed 9/11. A few remaining Texas International pilots still have a small CARP benefit.

As you might recall, United Airlines (UAL) filed for Chapter 11 federal bankruptcy protection on December 9, 2002. At the time, it was the sixth largest bankruptcy in American corporate history and also the longest to unwind. It took so long that Congress subsequently rewrote the bankruptcy code to include provisions that would deter "gaming" bankruptcy laws.

Finally, in May of 2005, the bankruptcy court approved United's plan to terminate the employee pensions, clearing the way for the largest corporate-pension default in American history.[1]

The Pension Benefit Guaranty Corporation (PBGC) provides a safety net for participants in private-sector defined-benefit plans by insuring participants' benefits under the plan. This federal corporation was established by the Employee Retirement Income Security Act (ERISA) of 1974 in order to give guaranteed "basic" benefits to participants in plans that are covered by the PBGC in the event that their employer-sponsored defined benefit plans become insolvent.

Ever since the PBGC terminated United's pension, senior Legacy-United pilots have been relegated to the PBGC benefit that's calculated based on their age and other inputs at the time of the pension freeze. For those not already retired, these residual benefits offer annuities to be paid out at age 60 or later that cannot be converted to a lump sum. In most cases the PBGC benefit falls far short of the pilot's accrued benefit at the time of the A-Plan termination.

THREE PENSION DISTRIBUTION OPTIONS FOR CAL PILOTS

Although a few, small, residual pensions exist from Texas International and other long-gone mergers, only the Continental Pilot's Retirement Plan (CPRP) remains to provide any meaningful benefits to the bulk of the senior legacy Continental pilots.

For Legacy Continental Airline (CAL) pilots that have earned benefits under CPRP, there are three distribution options available: (1) Annuity, (2) Lump Sum and, (3) Deferred Payment, what I call "Retire and Suspend," which is a rare but potentially valuable way to maximize the value of your pension.

1. THE DEFINED BENEFIT ANNUITY OPTION (A-PLAN)

An annuity is the core benefit provided by any defined benefit plan. Simply put, a defined benefit is the annuity that is calculated as a function of your age, longevity and income. At Continental, that calculation was frozen when "Contract 2002" was implemented in April of 2005.

For a pilot retiring at age 65, the PBGC maximum monthly guarantee for 2014 was as high as $4,943 per month. Few pilots have "frozen" benefits that high. The annuity is a relatively safe option. Moreover, the American Airlines bankruptcy and the fact that United has already *PBGC'd* its legacy pension, suggests that it's very unlikely the government would permit the new United to walk away from its frozen CPRP.

Like most defined benefit plans, CPRP is not indexed to inflation. That's a big issue when you consider that most people who are 65 today have a good chance of living at least 20 more years. As difficult as it might be to believe, today's life spans keep surprising insurance companies. If you're already 65, the odds are even, if not better, that you'll live past age 85.

At a 3 percent rate of inflation, which is close to the Fed's "unspoken" target, your annuity will be only 50 percent of what it is today 20 years down the road. If inflation is lower, your annuity will be more. If there's runaway inflation at some point in time in your lifetime, then your money is going to depreciate very rapidly.

The upshot: Inflation, not the PBGC, is clearly the biggest risk that faces your annuity.

Some will argue that you could take your lump sum and get a commercial annuity. **Here are three reasons why I *don't* recommend taking your lump sum to buy a commercial annuity.**

1. The PBGC guarantee is better than the guarantee that any commercial company can give you.

2. For it to be an inflation-adjusted annuity, you're going to get a whole lot less initial retirement income than you would have gotten from the airline's pension plan.

3. Features unique to a corporate pension practically guarantee that you'll get more money for the same scenario than you could ever get in a commercial annuity.

One benefit of the annuity, of course, is that unlike the lump sum, the annuity is a known quantity. At our firm, when we create plans for clients who are approaching retirement, we always run the numbers using the annuity. That's because we already know what the annuity will be. We know the problems with the annuity. We know that the annuity is not inflation adjusted. What we *don't* know is what the lump sum will be. That's because the lump sum is interest-rate sensitive.

The lump sum, of course, is somewhat of an unknown variable until you retire. This is not to say we recommend against taking a lump sum payout. Only that, for planning purposes, it's prudent to plan for an annuity and to make the lump sum decision when approaching your final retirement date.

Therefore, the key advantage of the annuity is that it leaves less room for error in your retirement plan. After running the numbers, if it seems that your annuity (plus Social Security) is barely going to be enough for you to live on, then the odds are good that you're going to be better off with the annuity than you'll be with the lump sum. Why? Because taking the lump sum requires you to take a lower initial payout than an annuity can offer. That's because you are now responsible for portfolio risk, inflation risk, political risk and "advisor" risk.

There are a number of annuity benefit options, providing a survivor benefit that's based on a percentage of the employee's benefit: 50 percent, 66 percent, 75 percent or 100 percent survivor benefit. There are two schools of thought on which is the preferred option. You can assume your surviving spouses annuity need will be less than the combined benefit. Alternatively, you can provide a full (100 percent) survivor benefit with just a slight reduction in the annuity. The choice is largely driven by two factors: The difference in expected longevity; the greater the difference, the greater the value of a 100 percent survivor benefit. The second factor is inflation protection. If one assumes a 3 percent inflation component, then a 100 percent survivor benefit will pay a 50 percent benefit in real dollars in 20 years. Either way, we get to the same conclusion: For most pilots selecting an annuity benefit, the 100 percent survivor benefit is optimal.

You can easily predict your estimated longevity by going to the website www.LivingTo100.com. This website combines medical and family information along with your age and some demographic inputs to generate a fairly accurate longevity projection.

There are also what's known as 'period certain' benefits whereby benefits are paid for a specified period (usually ten or twenty years). For married pilots, I discourage this option unless a unique scenario exists that will replace the lost income at the end of the defined annuity period. However, this option enables you to bequeath the benefit to a non-spouse beneficiary, which may be attractive to single pilots.

With the exception of the 'period certain' annuity option, the key disadvantage to the annuity is that there's no remainder for your estate. As noted, I only recommend the 'period certain' annuity option for single pilots. In all other cases, if you opt for an annuity, that's it. When you pass away and/or your spouse passes away, there's no money left for your estate. The lump sum is another alternative that we'll discuss next.

2. The Lump Sum Option (A-Plan)

The lump sum option is considered an alternate method of payment. The plan document permits taking the calculated present value of the annuity that's available to the retiree and converting it to a lump sum payout and is the actuarial equivalent of the annuity. This "present value of an annuity" (PVA) calculation is the source of much confusion and misunderstanding.

Essentially, the PVA is the current value of a set of future cash flows, given a specified discount rate. The rate used is a composite rate described by the Pension Protection Act of 2006.

Consequently, the key determinants of the size of your lump sum are:

1. The annuity you would otherwise receive.

2. The composite interest rate used to calculate the lump sum.

3. The period of time you would otherwise receive the annuity.

The lump sum option faces a number of risks including sensitivity to interest rates. The lump sum behaves like a bond. It's susceptible to rising interest rates. The interest rate sensitivity of the lump sum payout is approximately 8.8 percent per for every 1 percent change in interest rates. So, if interest rates spike 1 percent, then your lump sum payout would decrease up to 8.8 percent.

What many investors have trouble understanding is that as you age, your lump sum can decrease in value even if interest rates remain constant. After age 60, this decrease in the lump sum can become more pronounced. Why? Because your annuity is based on the present value of a *series* of equal periodic payments. In this case, the shorter the series (due to remaining longevity) the less your lump sum is worth.

Example: At age 65, if your annuity is $4,000 per month and you have an actuarial life expectancy of 23 more years, then the present value of that annuity, discounted by interest rates, is the value of the lump sum. As you approach age 66 or 67, there are fewer years left for you to receive that annuity, therefore you will receive a lower lump sum. Many pilots over 60 with frozen lump sums complain, "Why is my lump sum decreasing even when we don't account for interest rates going up?" That's because there are fewer years left for which you would receive that annuity in retirement.

The need to protect retirement income from inflation

Another challenge is that the cash income we derive from our lump sum must be protected from inflation. This can be achieved if you have your portfolio invested in a properly designed asset allocation that is expected to exceed the rate of inflation for you to earn an inflation-protected annuity.

NOTE: In Chapter 10, we will discuss how you can accomplish this goal via Advanced Cash Management™ and a disbursement policy.

Why does the sum have to exceed the rate of inflation? Because any asset allocation that is not purely in TIPS or Treasuries is going to have a bad year sooner or later.

What are TIPS? Treasury Inflation Protected Securities are essentially risk-free bonds, the principal of which is inflation adjusted, providing a capital gains component that offsets the loss of purchasing power over time.

How safe is the lump sum?

This is the most frequently asked question at our firm.

The PBGC is very unlikely to terminate CPRP.

Under the Pension Protection Act of 2006 (PPA '06) there is no requirement for CPRP to maintain any set funding level in order to pay out lump sums. The lump sum could go away temporarily due to a liquidity shortfall (calculated quarterly) or if the plan experienced a distressed termination.

In a liquidity shortfall scenario you can 'retire and suspend', described later, to protect your benefit options.

CARP and CPRP are funded under different funding rules as a result of PPA'06 and the company continues to fund both plans with more funds than required by current law. Since the two plans funding requirements and required interest rates used to calculate the funding levels are different, it is not possible to compare the funding levels of two plans. The company has demonstrated its commitment to continue funding these two plans as required by law.

The Air Line Pilots Association (ALPA) is highly motivated to maintain a vigilant watch on the funding status. ALPA receives monthly statements and forecast contributions for the plan year. Both the company and ALPA actuaries review the forecast payments and funding levels to make certain there are not liquidity shortfalls. They are aware of both the plan's funding and expenditures.

If you receive a lump sum, what do you do with it?

Now let's assume you've made it to retirement with your lump sum intact. What now? You have a couple of choices: You can roll your lump sum over to a qualified retirement account. That could be your 401(k), Rollover IRA or a qualified insurance annuity. These are your primary choices.

It's important to make sure that if you roll over to an IRA, you roll it into a *separate Rollover IRA*—separate from any non-rollover account, not a Traditional IRA.

What's the difference between a Traditional IRA and a Rollover IRA? On the surface, they look exactly the same, but the difference has to do with their level of ERISA protection in case of bankruptcy. A change to the bankruptcy laws a few years ago altered the asset protection available to Traditional IRAs in many states. At the federal level, asset protection is limited to the first $1 million of your Traditional IRA. A Rollover IRA maintains ERISA asset protection as long as it's not commingled with other accounts.

Is there an advantage to using a 401(k) versus a Rollover IRA?

If you're going to roll over your 401(k) to a large Wall Street broker-age firm or to a firm that's going to sell mostly proprietary funds, then the odds are that you probably will enjoy better options and lower costs in your Charles Schwab 401(k).

If you're going to roll your 401(k) over to a retail Rollover IRA at Charles Schwab, there's still a slight difference in cost structure of the 401(k) Personal Choice Retirement Account or PCRA. The cost impact should be minimal as long as you're not day-trading your account. Efficient Wealth Management has negotiated additional discounts that are more comparable to what the PCRA transactional costs are within the 401(k).

WHAT IS THE PCRA?

The Personal Choice Retirement Account (PCRA) is a brokerage ac-count option within the PRAP. It is created as an investment option, like any other option available. Once funds are in the PCRA they can be managed by you, or your advisor, independently of the traditional 401(k) options. Handle with caution: Data suggests that individual investors, when utilizing a brokerage window as a trading platform, significantly underperform the more traditional 401(k) options available. However, the PCRA also enables a skilled advisor to create a more sophisticated asset allocation, working within the context of a holistic plan that might include outside assets. The PCRA is a valuable tool, but one that should be treated with respect.

Why would you want to roll your 401(k)? Assuming that you're working with a firm that doesn't have a significant cost disadvantage, dealing with the trustee of a 401(k) when you want to make transfers and dealing with withdrawal changes, among other things, can be laborious. It can include filling out a form, mailing it, waiting three weeks for it to happen, and meeting other criteria.

Many 401(k) plans limit withdrawals to a specific percentage of the account. At legacy CAL, for instance, the trustees would not allow you to withdraw more than 10 percent of the total account value in any given year. We are researching to see if this applies to the new United PRAP.

In most cases, it is unusual for this to be an issue. You may be thinking, "Well why would I want to take out more than the limit?" You actually might have a very good reason to do so if you have substantial assets elsewhere, and/or you have a relatively small lump sum. You may be under age 59½ and the 401(k) is your only accessible qualified retirement plan. So you may want to get that money out first. There are a number of unusual scenarios that might cause this to happen.

When should you take a lump sum instead of an annuity?

The advantages of getting a lump sum have to do with control and your estate. Consider your estate. Managed correctly, a lump sum that's moved into a Rollover IRA can be inherited by your heirs and can be disbursed over their lifetimes.

That said, control is a double-edged sword. With this strategy you have control over choices now and those choices may be made with or without professional assistance. However, if you get the strategy wrong, there's the risk of running out of money. Managing your lump sum can be complex, whether you do it yourself or do it with a professional advisor.

There are additional risks involved: portfolio (or market) risk, inflation risk, and advisor risk (which includes product risk).

Let's talk about **market and inflation risk** first. Everyone is aware that the stock market can drop 20 percent in a relatively short period of time; but they're less aware that inflation could hit three percent, four percent, even five percent. Three percent inflation, over 20 years, will cut the real, inflation-adjusted, value of your income in half.

There is also **interest rate risk**. A "conservative" portfolio invested in, say, 60 percent fixed income (bonds), is not so conservative when one considers the investor's exposure to interest rate risk. If interest rates go up substantially, the portion of the portfolio that is invested in fixed income will lose value.

You also have **advisor risk** and **product risk.** For example, suppose you buy a guaranteed annuity that turned out to be more advantageous for the insurance company than it was for you, the investor or suppose you pick a bad advisor. Suppose you don't get this figured out until you've lost 30 percent to 40 percent of your principal and/or income. You have to make a massive cut in your living standard. Again, there's a significant risk to taking a lump sum.

3. Deferred Payment: The Retire and Suspend Option (A-Plan)

A little-known strategy is to retire, but not to take your pension right away. Otherwise known as the deferred payment, I call this "retire and suspend." This advanced strategy for the A-Plan works best if you retire early. Why? Because there's greater time for the assumed interest rate to compound your benefit. It also requires that you keep a close eye on the status and valuation of your lump-sum if your intent is to cash out at some point in the future.

What happens if you retire and don't claim your pension? Many pilots don't know this, but the minute you retire from the airline the annuity obligation to you grows in value over time based on specific criteria.

The first thing to understand is that the annuity itself is what grows.

As you age, given a shorter expected remaining lifespan, you'll receive a higher monthly annuity benefit to match your retirement age actuarial benefit. In essence, this is a boost in monthly income but not a boost in lifetime value. In fact, because the boost in deferred income is in nominal dollars, there's a slight annual loss in real lifetime value of about 3 percent per year, but only for those amounts that are deferred. In reality, the aggregate loss in purchasing power due to inflation that's specific to this strategy will be small. Also, because the lump sum, if elected, is the net present value of an annuity, it does not benefit from this portion of the benefit increase.

However, an additional source of annuity growth is the assumed interest rate applied to the growth of the plan assets. This is currently 8.5 percent[2]. Like much of corporate America, the airlines have come up with what are often considered ridiculous projections for their portfolio growth. Why? So they can put less money into their pension plans. However, and this is where the real benefit is, once retired, those ridiculous projections are now applied to your deferred payment. This is a real return, not just an actuarial adjustment.

The combined effect of the actuarial boost and the application of the assumed interest rate is typically in excess of 13 percent per year growth in deferred annuity income. This should not be confused with a return on investment. The return-on-investment for this strategy is closer to 8.0 percent after factoring nominal purchasing power loss.

When discussing this strategy, I often mention the portfolio insurance benefit. That is, if your retirement nest egg is negatively affected by market events, this is a nice source of added diversification for your retirement income.

However, if you're hoping to boost your future lump sum payout, the growth in the lump sum starts at a little under 8.5 percent and starts to decrease after you reach a point because the lump sum is still the net present value of your annuity given your remaining life expectancy (which has an increasingly negative impact on your lump sum as you age).

That's the why. Is it worth it? An 8.0 percent return on investment with added risk protection by the PBGC along with portfolio insurance benefits is a good deal.

How best to execute this strategy? That depends on your objective. If you intend to take the annuity, defer the annuity to 70 while either living on qualified plan (401k/PRAP) assets or, better yet, taxable assets and converting qualified assets to Roth IRA plans.

If you intend to take the lump sum you are facing counterbalancing forces that increase over time (and therefore reduce the deferral value over time). Monitor the lump sum on a semi-annual basis and when the growth rate has fallen below an acceptable rate (no later than age 70) then roll your funds to the 401(k) or a Rollover IRA.

Are there any pitfalls to this strategy? If you're single or married with less than a 100 percent survivor benefit there's the risk that you will lose lifetime value due to an early death. Remember, you have a 50/50 chance of reaching your actuarial life expectancy. To protect against this risk, you might consider a level term insurance policy. Because these rapidly become more expensive past 60, you would want to anticipate your use of this strategy and purchase an appropriate policy well before retirement if feasible.

An important note about Defined Benefit (CPRP) Pension death benefits

When a pilot retires, he or she is faced with two types of death benefits. The first death benefit affects the pension if the pilot dies prior to retirement. In that case, there's a 50 percent annuity to the pilot's spouse and all other forms of benefit. When the pilot dies after retirement, there's a spousal benefit that kicks in if the pilot took an annuity. The spouse will receive the value option (50, 66, 75, 100 percent) selected at retirement.

Why is this important? Because if you're dying, and have a significant defined benefit, you need to consider retirement.

You care about your family. It's very important for employees who have heirs they care about to have some form of general power of attorney that permits your spouse to "retire" you in the event of a tragic, terminal scenario (preferably a "springing" power of attorney, so if there's an estranged relationship the spouse can't do horrible damage).

What do we mean by a springing power of attorney? It means that three to five medical conditions must exist. Usually, this refers to conditions in which you can't take care of yourself and for which a doctor has signed off.

CAT. II: Defined Contribution Plans

A defined contribution (DC) plan is a retirement plan in which a certain amount (or percentage of income) is set aside each year by a company for the benefit of the employees. You can also contribute to a defined contribution plan. As a plan beneficiary, there are restrictions about when and how you can withdraw your accumulated funds without incurring penalties.

There is no way to know how much the plan will ultimately give the employee upon retiring. The *amount* that's contributed is "defined," but the benefit is not.

UAL Defined Contribution Plans

So let's get into United's defined contribution plans. We have a lot going on. We have a 401(k) to which you can contribute $17,500 per year (as of 2014), plus another $5,500 if you're over 50. That's $23,000 per year.

One option available is to make Roth 401(k) contributions in lieu of Traditional 401(k) contributions.

The Roth 401(k) is a wonderful investment opportunity. Future earnings will never be subject to income tax (though at some point they will likely be stealth-taxed through indirect taxation based on aggregate retirement savings, reduced social security or some similar measure). In addition, the Roth is exempt from required minimum distributions at 70 (thereby forcing the depletion of the account as you age).

I strongly recommend this option for younger, lower-paid pilots. If only to start the five-year seasoning that's required of all Roth accounts.

Which is preferable? As a general rule of thumb, once your marginal tax bracket hits 25 percent, you're generally better off making Traditional 401(k) contributions. After deductions and exemptions, this tax bracket can be estimated at about $100,000 AGI for a married couple. For more precision, you may review the tax tables at IRS.gov.

In addition to the 401(k) options that are available, we have the B-Plan from Legacy Continental to which the company was adding 16 percent. That can be a great deal depending on your age. If you're in your 30s or 40s, that will compound substantially. If you're 63, well, there's not a whole lot that compound interest can do for you.

United has recently consolidated the above plans and Legacy United's 'C-Plan' into a new plan called The Pilot Retirement Account Plan (PRAP). The original concept was for United to take the 401(k), the B-Plan and the C-Plan, and turn them into a single account in which you can put your money and they can add contributions. It was intended to be a simple and elegant replacement for the three.

However, Legacy United's pilots wanted to keep their C-Plan as a representation of their terminated A-Plan. There's no current economic rationale for this added complexity; however, the UAL MEC has elected to retain this structure to preserve their future retirement negotiating position with regard to Legacy United's terminated A-Plan.

Now, the PRAP has the original 401(k), B-Plan and a new C-Plan. The 16 percent B-Plan contributions are now divided between the B-Plan (9 percent) and the C-Plan (7 percent). How does this affect you? If you're currently using the PCRA to manage your retirement assets, you now have the potential for substantially increased complexity if trying to manage a cost-efficient asset allocation across multiple accounts.

One nice feature of the PRAP that is a legacy of the original intent to simplify is that you can setup a single PCRA account to accept contributions from the 401k, B- and C-Plan. We're using single PCRA accounts for new clients and expect to consolidate existing clients over time.

A closer look at the PRAP can be found in the Appendix section of this book.

In summary, defined contribution plans are the wave of the future, whether you like it or not. I recently read a post online about how a certain labor group was looking to get defined benefit plans back. There is a concern that the history of these plans does not elicit confidence in their future. However, so long as the maximum benefit is designed to stay below PBGC benefit protection limits and given the lifetime income diversification of these plans, there is a strong argument for keeping them in the mix.

A brief discussion of the executive SERP plan can be found in the Appendix of this book.

Defined contribution plans may be complex, but they can grow and they can't be taken from you. Challenges are created by wealth in a defined contribution plan. You have a real problem once you're retired—how do you get your money out? How do you disperse the money during retirement? What's the most durable strategy? To help you answer those types of questions, see the Advanced Cash Management™ and Disbursement Policies section of Chapter 10.

CAT. III: Hybrid Insurance Savings Plans

The RHA VEBA

A Retiree Healthcare Account (RHA) is funded with employer money for the purpose of paying retirees and eligible dependents out-of-pocket health care expenses and premiums. A Voluntary Employees' Beneficiary Association (VEBA) is essentially a pooled tax-advantaged trust that's designed to provide benefits. Certain tax opportunities exist with this type of trust, but it's important to understand the concept of the pool.

What are the tax opportunities of this program? Funds put into the VEBA are pre-tax dollars.

Why would you want an RHA VEBA? Essentially the problem is that retiree medical expenses are becoming increasingly onerous. We expect that the average United Airlines retired pilot could spend as much as an estimated $6,000 to $7,000 dollars per year on company-provided supplemental healthcare premiums, deductibles and co-pays. Additional medical expenses will include Medicare Part B, prescription drug co-pays and other long-term care needs. The VEBA can be used to pay for these expenses, but only after an employee retires. Once you're retired, you can use the VEBA to pay for medical expenses, long-term care, insurance premiums and reimbursement of health care insurance. Essentially anything that a flex savings account would pay for, a VEBA can pay for.

One item that the VEBA can cover that's not covered by the flex savings account is qualified long term care premiums. This is valuable not only because of the need for long term care, but also because many pilots with Tri-Care or other similar coverage due to their spouse will find that their VEBA accounts are otherwise overfunded.

The next question is about how your account is funded. On the surface it seems you don't have control over the account, but, technically you do, through a "back door" mechanism for want of a better term. How so? You can't say, "I want to put this extra money into a VEBA." At this time, forfeited vacation can be treated as an employer contribution to the 401(k), causing you to reach the 415(c) limit sooner. The benefit is that once the 415(c) limit is reached, B-Plan contributions now spill over to the VEBA.

I've included some detailed scenarios describing how you can manipulate your RHA VEBA contributions if your income is between $210,000 and $260,000. These scenarios have been added to the Appendix.

Finally, can your estate inherit the VEBA RHA account if you die? No.

Again, we get back to the concept of a pooled trust. This money belongs to the trust and it is for your benefit and your eligible dependents. Though you make indirect contributions while employed (company contributions, PRAP spillover amounts and $1 per pay hour), your share of this trust is pro rata. This is significant because you cannot bequeath it; however, after you die, eligible dependents can submit reimbursement until your share is depleted. However, if there is no surviving qualified dependent (ref. Appendix), any remaining account balance is going to be forfeited for the benefit of the remaining plan participants.

Health Savings Accounts

A Health Savings Account (HSA) is an account created for individuals who are covered under high-deductible health plans (HDHPs) so they can save for medical expenses that HDHPs do not cover. Contributions are made into the account by the individual or the individual's employer and are limited to a maximum amount each year. The 2013 tax year contribution limit was $6,550 for family coverage and there was a $1,000 catch up for people age 55 or older. If you're planning ahead, the catch up has not changed for 2014 contributions.

The contributions are invested over time and can be used to pay for qualified medical expenses, which include most medical care such as dental, vision and over-the-counter drugs.

The HSA account has three major tax advantages:

1. Money contributed into the account is tax deductible.

2. The money grows tax-free.

3. Withdrawals are tax-free if they are for qualified medical expenses.

To qualify for an HSA account, you must have coverage from a high-deductible health plan and you must **not** be enrolled in Medicare **nor** be listed as a dependent on another person's tax return. Note: You are not eligible for an HSA if you have Tricare

Making contributions through your employer's payroll can provide added tax benefits: HSA contributions are not subject to the Federal Insurance Contributions Act (FICA) and the Federal Unemployment Tax Act (FUTA) taxes, which amounts to a typical savings of 7.65 percent but could also reduce one's exposure to the new Affordable Care Act supplemental Medicare tax of 3.8 percent!

United provides a company contribution of $1,500 per year. That's free money!

Think of an HSA as a hybrid Traditional IRA/Roth IRA. The Roth IRA is great, but you can't deduct the contributions. A Traditional IRA is great, except that your future withdrawals are taxed as ordinary income instead of at the more favorable capital gains rates.

An HSA enables you to take advantage of a deduction for the money that goes in and, if you use that money in retirement for long-term care, medical expenses, or any number of qualified expenses that are large and likely to hit you, then you're not going to pay tax on those withdrawals.

Another significant difference between an HSA and a RHA VEBA or a FSA is that if you don't use it, you DON'T lose it. Your HSA is in your estate. It does go to your heirs. *(Ref. Appendix for more information)*

There is a catch, however. If you don't have the cash flow to pay for your medical care (and an HSA is usually associated with a high deductible health care plan), then you will need to pay for your medical care by dipping into this account. In this case, you might as well just use the health care reimbursement account (FSA) and a lower deductible insurance policy.

Using your HSA in retirement

There are many medical costs to plan for in retirement from long-term care to Medicare premiums and many others. During retirement, funds in an HSA are a great way to pay for these expenses tax-free. Some of these expenses may include qualified medical, prescription, dental, and vision expense; long-term care premiums; Medicare parts A and B premiums and out-of-pocket expenses; Medicare co-insurance; and part D prescription drug premiums and co-insurance.

Another significant benefit for retirees age 65 and older is that HSA funds can be used for every day spending and are taxed only at your income tax rate, which will likely be lower than when you were working.

How much do you save?

We recommend building up your HSA account to as much as $150,000 to $200,000, depending on your family's conceivable medical and long-term care expenses. You may reduce this figure by the balance held in your RHA VEBA account.

A case for additional savings exists if you intend to use this account for retirement income, reducing the draw on other tax qualified accounts that you intend to bequeath.

Flex Spending Account

A Flex Spending Account (FSA) is a type of savings account that provides the account holder with specific tax advantages. Set up by an employer for an employee, an FSA allows employees to contribute a portion of their regular earnings to pay for "qualified" expenses, such as medical expenses or dependent care expenses.

One of the key benefits of a flexible spending account is that the funds contributed to the account are deducted from the employee's earnings *before* they are made subject to payroll taxes. So, regular contributions to an FSA can significantly lower an employee's annual tax liabilities.

There are limits to how much can be contributed to an FSA account per year. For medical expense FSA accounts, the limit is $2,500 per year, while the specified limit for dependent care accounts is $5,000 per year.

The FSA is often confused with a Health Savings Account. It is important to note that *the medical expense FSA can only be used if you do not have an HSA*. Be careful to use it in year of, not year after, when switching from FSA to HSA, to avoid inadvertently violating this rule.

The FSA is something you should use if you want to save on the taxes and you don't want to take advantage of the HSA. Unfortunately there's a downside to the FSA—the value of your time. You have to submit claims. United provides FSA debit cards. Personally, I'm not a fan of these debit cards, because you have to track receipts in case any of your claims are denied. However, others swear by them. To mitigate the hassle of justifying claims retroactively, you may limit their use to rarely challenged expenses such as office visits and prescription co-pays. Debit cards can become more administrative work than simply submitting a claim online about once every 90 days for five or six receipts at a time.

If you have the time and/or someone to run the FSA, then do it. The value of a Captain's time managing this account maybe more than the tax benefit of a $2,500 FSA. On the other hand, the value of the Captain's spouse or significant other's time may be worth the effort.

Regardless of the hassle factor, though, you should ALWAYS plan to use the FSA in your last year of employment. Why? Because you can make in-service withdrawals up to the full benefit for the year even if you retire early in the year. It's important that the withdrawals be made prior to retirement; however, because your contributions are annualized, this is a great way to withdraw more than you contribute in your retirement year.

MetLife VUL Insurance

One new benefit, first offered in 2014, is the MetLife VUL Insurance Policy. This policy has two components: A renewable, portable life insurance policy and a tax-deferred investment option.

The renewable/portable feature is attractive if you cannot get quality level term life insurance due to some pre-existing condition. Otherwise, it's an expensive albatross of a product and we only recommend it when alternative underwriting is not available for a client who needs life insurance.

How do we define portable? It means the insurance can be carried into retirement. In retirement, the premiums are direct billed by MetLife. The rates increase with age. In retirement, coverage can be decreased and never increased. However, the investment portfolio can be used to pay premiums.

The tax deferred investment option is of little value. Investing after-tax dollars into a product that will most assuredly have higher costs and, therefore, lower returns than many equivalent indexed offerings elsewhere makes little sense—especially since the higher cost option will result in higher ordinary income tax on future investment gains.

Some would argue that VUL insurance offers better asset protection than a taxable account. However, if this protection is important, then you should have an umbrella insurance policy. If you have more than $1 million in non-qualified investment assets, then those assets should be protected by an asset protection entity.

We work closely with clients who have asset protection needs, but this advanced planning activity is beyond the scope of this book.

Profit Sharing Elections

It's important to discuss the effects of United's profit sharing plan and the elections available for both the PRAP and the RHA VEBA.

All United pilots participate in the company profit sharing plan. It's not elective. For profit sharing based on the years 2014 and beyond, the company profit sharing plan shall be funded with 10 percent of pre-tax profit up to a pre-tax margin of 6.9 percent, plus 20 percent of pre-tax profit in excess of a pre-tax margin of 6.9 percent.

Special and unusual items shall be excluded from pre-tax profit when making the calculations.

Set yourself a reminder to update your profit sharing elections around January 15th of each year. Typically you need to decide if you want the profit sharing to be deposited into your PRAP or to be paid, and taxed, in cash.

When would you want to deposit profit sharing to the PRAP? You should elect for the PRAP if you cannot fully fund your 401(k), for whatever reason, and/or if you want the funds to overflow into your RHA VEBA. In most other cases, take the cash and invest it in debt reduction or tax-efficient but taxable investments.

CAT. IV: Retiree Medical Benefits and Traditional Insurance Options

Retiree Medical Benefits

The new Pilot Contract includes new retiree medical benefits that are of significant value.

A covered pilot is one who retires on or after the effective date of the new contract, and who is at least age 50 and has completed at least 10 years of service. Eligible dependents receive before-Medicare benefits coverage or after-Medicare benefits coverage. The coverage is not free and may be dropped at will. A retiree may choose from among the retiree medical benefits coverage options and coverage levels available.

ALERT: If you fail to accept this benefit at retirement, or you drop this benefit, maybe because your spouse has medical benefits, you CANNOT enroll at a later date without proof of coverage during the entire period not enrolled. Be careful to maintain evidence of proof of coverage. Most group insurers provide a certificate of coverage annually (often in PDF form and located online).

The option to 'enroll and suspend' exists; along with the option to suspend coverage. However, this is a subtle difference from failing to elect and/or dropping the coverage that must be handled with care to prevent the permanent loss of this great benefit.

Retired pilots who elect medical benefits coverage for themselves and their eligible dependents are required to make contributions for each month of coverage in amounts determined on the basis of coverage option and coverage tier elected.

Before-Medicare Medical Benefits: When eligible and during any annual enrollment, a retired pilot may elect from among the same, required or optional coverage options. Except for any HMO, the required contribution for each month of coverage under a particular before-Medicare coverage option and coverage tier elected is equal to a percentage of the total projected cost of that coverage option and coverage tier, based on the pilot's years of service, further described in the appendix.

After-Medicare Medical Benefits: When eligible and during any subsequent annual enrollment, a retired pilot may elect from among one or more supplemental plans to Medicare offered by the company. Eligible individuals must pay a monthly contribution for the cost of after-Medicare coverage. The monthly contribution is equal to the total projected cost of such after-Medicare coverage for the calendar year, per person, minus a company contribution equal to $90 per month per person covered.

I've saved a discussion of retiree medical benefits available to the deceased pilot's survivors and dependents for the Appendix section of this book.

HCTC | *Stay covered.* **Health Coverage Tax Credit:** This is an oft-overlooked medical tax credit made available to those pilots whose pension has been taken over by the PBGC and are not covered by Tricare or Medicare. It does require reauthorization by Congress. In 2013, the HCTT covered 72.5 percent of qualified health insurance premiums. The tax credit expired at the end of 2013 and its future is uncertain. However, you can still file for the credit in 2013 using IRS Form 8885.

A note about Medicare and Social Security

Once you turn 65, you should consider the need to apply for Medicare. For the vast majority of pilots who have younger spouses, taking Social Security at full retirement age or even at age 70 is optimal and will result in the greatest end-of-life value.

Let's say you're going to take Social Security at age 67. If medical insurance is available to you, but you do not maintain continuous group coverage, then your Medicare premium will increase if you defer Medicare past age 65.

As such, it is important that you enroll in Medicare at age 65 if you qualify and do not have any other safe harbor health insurance alternatives. If you have enrolled for Social Security benefits then you are automatically enrolled in Medicare. If you have not, you have to notify the Social Security Administration.

Most people don't know enough about Social Security and Medicare to make informed decisions about those programs, so it's essential that you work with a skilled financial professional to make these critical and frequently irreversible decisions.

Traditional insurance options

As a United pilot, you get major medical, dental and vision insurance. These are fairly good policies, similar to those found at most large corporations. The math is pretty simple. If you can get a better policy through your spouse, do it. Keep in mind that if something goes wrong and you have a "life event," you can switch back to the airline's plan.

Also, there are two types of life insurance. One is Variable Universal Life (VUL), mentioned previously. There is also Company Provided Basic Group Life Insurance. Basic group life insurance is equal to the base pay for a pilot.

Note: Something that's not well understood is that the premium value of any basic life insurance that's in excess of $50,000 actually shows up in your W2 statement as taxable income. There's really not anything you can do about it.

Possibly the most important coverage, after major medical, is Pilot Disability (Loss of License) insurance. The benefit is both affordable and subsidized to the tune of 65 percent by the company. That means, you are gaining much more in value than paying for the product. This benefit is capped at $8,000 per month ($96,000 per year), tax-free (if paid with post-tax dollars). Horror stories exist of young pilots needing this coverage having foregone it because they perceived they were in good health or not at risk. It's a simple recommendation: Get it and pay for it with post-tax dollars.

Finally, one type of insurance that pilots too often overlook is Accident Insurance. United offers a great policy. It used to be called Accidental Death and Dismemberment. For less than $10 per month—the cost of a few lattes at Starbucks—you can have $500,000 worth of coverage. **I cannot overstate the importance of getting this coverage**. It means you are protected if you are the victim of a severe injury that makes it impossible for you ever to work again, and requires you to get specialized care and attention. It's rare that a policy can be so valuable that we recommend it without reservation.

Are there any guarantees? A word about Guaranteed Minimum Withdrawal Benefit (GMWB) Variable Annuities

Finally, what about insurance annuities that have a guaranteed minimum withdrawal benefit? These are very common products. Chances are you've been invited to a lunch or dinner seminar to "learn all about them" along with a free meal or bottle of wine. Why are the hosts of these seminars so generous? Because variable annuities are very popular with commission sales people.

Let's follow the money: In insurance, a variable annuity with a guaranteed minimum withdrawal benefit is supposed to give you market upside with a guarantee for the return of principal over a seven to ten year window. But how good is that guarantee? As noted above, the product is popular with commission sales people, and they get paid well. For a $1 million policy, they're looking at maybe $50,000 in commission. That's probably enough to justify feeding 20 people for dinner. If you're a salesperson who sells two of these products—that's a $100,000 paycheck for one night's work. Not bad.

Just remember that, in the end, you're paying for these distribution costs out of future returns.

A full description of the mechanics of these products is beyond the scope of the body of this book, but I've added more detail in the Appendix. Suffice to say these products are expensive and the guarantee is easily replicated using far more cost efficient financial instruments. Remember: Follow the money.

In the next chapter, we'll review the overall investment process and explain how investment planning is at the core of how you achieve your top financial priorities.

---

1 Associated Press: "Timeline of United Airlines' Bankruptcy" as reported in *USA Today*, February 1, 2006.

2 Paul Jackson & William Fellers. "The UP-1984 A 'Unisex' Mortality Table for Non-Insured Pension Plans."

CHAPTER 4

THE STANDARD OPERATING PROCEDURES OF SUCCESSFUL INVESTING

INVESTMENT PLANNING IS THE FOUNDATION of a successful wealth management strategy for pilots and airline executives. The reason is obvious. You must position your wealth so it will grow over time and so it will be there when you need it to live the lifestyle you desire. An intelligent investment plan is central to achieving those goals. Without such an investment plan to help ensure the growth and preservation of your wealth, other more complex issues, such as estate planning and asset protection, become less relevant.

That is why the next five chapters of this book will focus on what we call the Standard Operating Procedures, or SOPs, of successful investing.

As you are well aware, there are numerous ways to position your investment capital—a quick look at any major financial website or TV program will give you myriad strategies for investing your money.

However, the vast majority of those methods are based on investment theories and beliefs that do not actually pan out in the real world. As a result, these strategies often lead to disappointing results for investors and a sense that the markets are rigged against you.

By contrast, I've found that if you follow these key rules below, you can maximize your ability to have a successful investment experience and to achieve your life goals.

SOP 1: Let the markets work for you

You do not have to spend your time and energy picking the perfect stocks or finding superstar fund managers to generate the returns you need to succeed. In fact, seeking perfect stocks or superstar fund managers will likely cause you to end up with subpar investment returns—results that could put your financial goals at risk. The reason: Financial markets work in ways that make them highly *efficient*. This means that it is extraordinarily difficult—some even say impossible—to outperform the market's overall rate of return. As explained in Chapter 5, the best approach is to invest in a manner that enables you to capture as much of the market return as possible. To put it another way, ***let the market work for you; don't work against the market***.

SOP 2: Take only the investment risks that pay off

The financial concept that risk and return are related is well known. It's the investment world's version of "nothing ventured, nothing gained." Indeed, taking additional risk *can* potentially generate stronger returns—*if* you take the right risks. Academic research reveals that there are three main types of investment risk that truly "pay off"—that is, they are risks that offer a strong potential to compensate investors who take them.

Those risks are (a) **market risk** (stocks outperform bonds over time), (b) **size risk** (stocks of small companies outperform stocks of larger firms), and (c) **value risk** (stocks with high book-to-market ratios outperform stocks with low book-to-market ratios). In addition, a new "dimension" of risk has recently been identified: **profitability** (shares of highly profitable companies can be expected to generate higher returns going forward than shares of less profitable companies). As explained in Chapter 6, investors who construct portfolios designed to capture these dimensions of risk can enhance their returns over time.

SOP 3: Diversify to reduce volatility and boost returns

No one—not even the world's smartest professional investors—can know precisely which types of investments will do well in a given month or year and which ones will do poorly. By building a truly well-diversified portfolio—one that consists of a wide variety of asset classes that do not rise and fall in concert with each other—you can reduce the swings in the value of your wealth. What's more, a well-diversified portfolio with relatively low volatility can actually help you generate a higher rate of return over time, thus, allowing you to build more wealth. That said, some methods of diversification are much more effective than others are at reducing volatility and enhancing returns. Chapter 7 will examine how to create properly diversified portfolios that accomplish those tasks.

SOP 4: Build asset class portfolios

Decisions about which specific investments to use for implementing your overall financial strategy, are crucial. What's more, making those choices can seem virtually impossible when you consider that in the U.S. alone, there are approximately 5,000 publicly traded companies[1], more than 7,700 mutual funds[2] and nearly 1,300 exchange-traded funds[3]. The good news: You can cut through the confusion of all those choices by focusing on asset class investments. As the name suggests, asset class investments are designed to help you capture the return of individual asset classes such as large-company growth stocks or short-term government bonds. Chapter 8 shows how asset class investments offer tremendous advantages—such as portfolio consistency, low costs and tax efficiency—that ultimately mean better returns and more money in your pocket.

SOP 5: Monitor closely, but act only when necessary

One of the most important parts of successful investing is to stay committed to your investment plan and to maintain your strategy. This can be surprisingly difficult, however, as there are many forces at work that can cause investors to break their discipline and take actions with their assets that are ultimately counterproductive. For example, there are many ways in which we tend to react emotionally, rather than rationally, about our money when major developments occur in the financial markets or the world at large. These emotional responses can severely hinder your ability to achieve your goals. Chapter 9 will offer solutions to maintain your carefully crafted investment strategy in good and bad market environments—including creating an investment policy statement to keep you on track and using rebalancing procedures to ensure that your portfolio retains your desired risk and return characteristics.

CONCLUSION

The rules described above form the overarching framework that we use to make investment decisions in collaboration with our clients. In the following chapters, you will come to understand each rule in more detail and see clearly how following each rule as part of a coordinated investment consulting plan will put you in the best possible position to achieve the results you need to enjoy a great and financially secure life.

1 World Federation of Exchanges (http://online.wsj.com/news/articles/SB1000142405270230485110457936327 2107177430)

2 Investment Company Institute (http://www.icifactbook.org/pdf/14_fb_table01.pdf)

3 Investment Company Institute (http://www.icifactbook.org/fb_ch3.html)

CHAPTER 5

LET THE MARKETS WORK FOR YOU

IF YOU ARE LIKE MANY INVESTORS, you are intrigued by the prospect of "beating the stock market"—earning returns that outpace well-known indices like the Dow Jones Industrial Average and the Standard & Poor's 500.

It's no wonder that many investors feel the urge to beat the market. After all, the message we get from advertisements and the media is that "more is better." Additionally, it may be tempting to own a top-gun portfolio that you can brag about to your pilot peers.

There's just one small problem: It is virtually impossible to beat the market consistently over time. In this chapter, you will come to see that this is the case because of the fundamental nature of the financial markets—the way the markets work effectively prevents investors from outpacing them often enough to come out ahead.

Believe it or not, this is great news for you as an investor. It means that you do not have to spend your time and energy picking the perfect stocks or finding superstar fund managers to generate the returns you need to reach your financial and life goals. In fact, doing so would be a "fool's errand." Instead, there is a much better alternative. You can adopt an approach to investing your hard-earned wealth that is designed to take full advantage of how the markets actually work and to capture the investment returns that are ripe for the picking.

TAKE WHAT YOU ARE OWED

Let's start by examining how the capital markets work (a capital market is any market in which investors trade securities). Capital markets operate in such a way that they deliver a rate of return to the people who invest in them. To put it simply, capital markets work—they do a great job of generating wealth over time. What's more, that wealth is literally sitting there waiting for each and every investor to grab his or her share of it.

Here's why. All publicly-traded companies are in business to make money, create wealth and increase in value. Although many companies go out of business, the vast majority generate wealth that grows over time (through higher profits each year, for example). If they didn't, our capitalist economy would have crumbled long ago. If you invest your money in shares of publicly-traded companies, you can claim ownership of a portion of that wealth. You literally share in the spoils of these firms' successes. They are yours for the taking!

The upshot: You can succeed as an investor simply by aligning yourself and your investment capital with the capital markets as a whole. Over time, you can have great confidence that companies will generate more and more wealth, which in turn will push their stock prices higher and higher. The capital markets will generate a rate of return.

The rate of return will differ depending on the particular market or "asset class" in which you invest. As seen in Figure 5.1, shares of small cap U.S. companies have generated an annual rate of return of 11.85 percent since 1926. Meanwhile the annual rate of return generated by stocks of the U.S. Market Index since 1926 has been 9.98 percent. The annual rate of return from the Long-Term Government Bond Index has been 5.53 percent during that period.

As you can see, there's quite a difference in returns realized by different asset classes.

Figure 5.1: Historical Rates of Return for Various Asset Classes

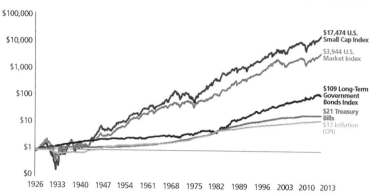

Source: Dimensional Fund Advisors. "Dimensions of Returns." Jan. 5 2013.

We'll show why different segments of the capital markets offer different returns in the next chapter. For now, all you need to know is that you as an investor can capture those rates of return. All you have to do is cast the widest net possible by investing in an entire market (or asset class). In doing so, you gain access to every single company that is generating wealth over time and you get to share in that wealth.

The concept of asset allocation goes part and parcel with adopting this approach. A number of studies have shown that the most importance factor when making investment decisions involves asset allocation. The asset classes you invest in (such as stocks, bonds, cash and more), combined with the percentage of your portfolio that you devote to each asset class and the method you use to gain and maintain access to those asset classes is what ultimately will have the largest impact on your future investment returns. In fact, one landmark study[1] revealed that asset allocation choices were responsible for a full 93 percent of the differences in returns among various portfolios being studied. In stark contrast, security selection—picking certain specific investments over others—was responsible for a mere 5 percent of the difference in returns between portfolios.

The upshot: Allocating assets among broad segments of the capital markets is by far the most important decision you need to make. As you will see later in this book, investing broadly in the capital markets is easily done using a select group of investments that ensure consistent exposure to various asset classes.

THE ALLURE OF "MORE"

Of course, many of you might be saying that you want to have more—that you'd rather generate returns that are higher than those offered to you by the broad capital markets. Really, why shouldn't you want that? If you can get more, go for it!

Investors who seek to beat the market must use active management strategies. The thought process is that instead of owning an entire market or asset class, active management investors try to select stocks that they think will generate exceptionally large gains, while also selling or avoiding certain stocks that they think will deliver losses or subpar gains. Active management investors may also attempt to shift their money in and out of entire asset classes at various times in an attempt to capture gains or avoid losses. For example, they might sell most or all of their stock holdings if they think the stock market overall is about to fall in value. Then they might move back into stocks right before they think the market is poised to rise in value.

Investors who pursue these strategies believe that stocks are often mispriced—that is, they trade at prices that are higher or lower than they should be. Therefore, the goal of active investors is to exploit the mispricing of stocks. If they can determine stock prices better than all the other investors in the marketplace—through hard work, intelligence, a unique insight or some other advantage—then they can theoretically spot opportunities that others miss and profit from their mistakes. For example, they might hope to find a stock that is trading at $10 but that they believe should be trading at $20. They buy the stock and wait for other investors to recognize the mispricing—at which point, investors bid up the stock price to $20 and those investors who bought at $10 can book a big profit.

THE BIG QUESTION: CAN YOU BEAT THE MARKET?

Sounds great, doesn't it? Obviously, if we can beat the market, we want to. However, the question that must be asked is: How likely is it that we can earn returns that are stronger than those offered to us by the capital markets?

Let's first consider what it might take for you to exploit any mispricings that might occur in the market. You would have to do what all the other investors out there do when they try to size up stock prices—you would read reports, analyze company financial statements and SEC filings, scour all the news you can find on various companies and learn all you can about the economy and various industries.

However, it may dawn on you that there are millions of other investors out there doing exactly what you are doing—and many of those investors are professionals with degrees in finance who devote themselves to analyzing stocks day in and day out. All of those investors are reading the exact same reports and news clips that you are—and probably more. What's more, many full-time investment professionals have access to resources that you don't (such as meetings with a company's management and competitors). In this environment, you'd have to ask yourself: What are the chances that I will obtain a piece of information so significant that it leads to a stock mispricing, but still goes unnoticed by all of these eagle-eyed investors paying such close attention to so many details? You'd have to admit that it's a bit like finding a $100 bill sitting on an empty seat in coach. It just doesn't happen very often.

However, let's say that you do somehow spot an anomaly that tells you a stock is mispriced, and you exploit it for profit. That's great. But how likely are you to find another one? Just as people don't tend to let $100 bills fall out of their pockets regularly, the market doesn't typically let stocks go unnoticed or become mispriced. What's more, the huge number of investors out there who are also looking for mispricings would practically erase your chances of finding more.

Therefore, you would want to attempt to beat the market only if you have the knowledge, insight and time needed to uncover market mispricings that the rest of your competitors—by which I mean all the other investors throughout the globe—overlook.

CAN A PROFESSIONAL MONEY MANAGER BEAT THE MARKET?

Of course, you're a busy pilot. Even though you might have plenty of downtime during some of your flights, you probably aren't going to spend that time—as well as your off hours and vacations—seeking out market-beating investments. Many of you have families and hobbies that you would rather focus on when you can.

Also, you're successful—you can afford to pay a professional to do the job for you. Certainly there are many options out there to choose from, including huge brokerage firms with scores of smart, hard-working analysts whose job it is to pick the right stocks and beat the market. Surely they can get the job done for you.

Not so fast. The research tells us that even the pros can't seem to outperform the capital markets' overall rate of return consistently over time. The statistics in Figure 5-2 are just two examples from among scores of studies over many decades showing how the pros fail to measure up to the markets:

ACTIVE MANAGEMENT UNDERPERFORMS

- The S&P 500 outperformed 86 percent of actively managed large-capitalization mutual funds during the three years through 2012, and outperformed 75 percent of large-cap funds during the five years through 2012.[2]

- The S&P Small Cap 600, an unmanaged index of small U.S. stocks, performed better than 83 percent of actively managed mutual funds that invest in small-cap stocks during both of those periods.[3]

- A study that examined performance over 32 years (1975-2006) found that, after expenses, less than 1 percent of actively managed mutual funds outperformed the market due to the managers' skill (i.e., their ability to identify and pick the right stocks).[4]

WHY IS IT SO DIFFICULT?

Clearly, the evidence shows that active management techniques that seek to beat the market have disappointing track records. Why is this? And could this dynamic change someday and make active management the superior approach?

Frankly, it's unlikely. The fact is, there are deeply embedded forces that work against active management. For example:

1. The future is unknowable. Wall Street, the financial media and other market participants love to peer into their crystal balls and tell investors that they know what is about to happen and to make buy and sell decisions based on those predictions. However, the fact is, no one—not even the most brilliant economist or investor—knows with certainty what the future will bring (see the sidebar on page ##). Yes, some market prognosticators will sometimes make a call that turns out to be true—but they're just as likely to turn around and make another call that is an abject failure. Luck is a big reason why most calls are accurate—and I think you'd agree that investing your hard earned wealth with someone you hope "gets lucky" with your money is no way to make smart financial decisions.

CONSIDER SOME OF THE CLASSIC PREDICTIONS GONE WRONG FROM THE LAST SEVERAL DECADES:

1. Respected Stanford economist Michael Boskin wrote in March 2009 that President Obama's "radicalism" would kill stocks. Just a few days later came the start of one of the longest-running bull markets in history.

2. The book *Dow 36,000: The New Strategy for Profiting from the Coming Rise in the Stock Market,* released in 1999 and co-authored by a former senior economist with the Federal Reserve, predicted that the stock market could reach that lofty level in just a few years. The Dow, at around 11,000 when the book appeared, closed at a record high of 11,723 the following January—and then plummeted 37 percent. It's still nowhere near 36,000.

3. The infamous August 1979 cover story in *Business Week* that warned investors to steer clear of stocks and stated "the stock market is just not where the action's at." Over the next decade, stocks would gain an amazing 17.5 percent annually.

By seeking to capture the market rate of return instead of trying to beat the market, you no longer have to base your decisions on predictions like those above—predictions that fail to pan out more often than not. Instead, you just have to believe that capitalism and the free market system will continue to work successfully—that, on balance, more companies will continue to grow and succeed than will shrink and fail—and align yourself with that growth.

2. The market prices stocks efficiently. Remember, huge numbers of professional and institutional investors work long hours every day to determine "accurate" prices for stocks, processing all the information that comes out about the economy and corporations as soon as it becomes available. The result is that the prices of stocks reflect all known information about those stocks at any given moment in time—that is, the market is highly efficient. When something changes, stock prices rise and fall quickly to reflect the effects of that new information. In this environment, it's virtually impossible for any one investor to have a sustainable advantage over another. Unless an investor has inside information that he uses to trade on illegally, everyone is essentially on the same page. That makes it tough for one investor to outperform another or to outperform the market rate of return.

Let's say for the sake of argument that the market is not efficiently priced, or that there are times when prices somehow do not reflect all the known information that's in the marketplace. It may be possible that such mispricings occur from time to time. However, it's one thing to spot mispricings and quite another thing to actually take advantage of them for profit.

To capture an inefficiency, you have to know exactly when to buy an investment and then, later, when to sell. If you get either decision wrong—say you buy a "loser" stock that you think is about to rise but instead remains in the dumps for another year, or sell a high-flying "overvalued" stock that goes on to soar another 100 percent—you will almost certainly end up earning a lower overall return in your portfolio than if you had just owned the entire market and accept its rate of return. Best advice: Act as if the market is efficient even if you think that's sometimes not the case.

3. Our emotions get the best of us. Remember from the discussion about behavioral finance in Chapter 2 that we all are hard-wired with tendencies that cause our emotions to overrule our brains at times. In particular, emotions such as fear and greed can cause investors to make the wrong decisions at exactly the wrong times—and these decisions can severely cut into their investment returns over time.

To witness this dynamic, we only need to look back to the market turmoil that occurred in 2008 and 2009. By early March 2009, the S&P 500 had fallen more than 50 percent from its record close less than two years earlier. At that time, it seemed like there was nothing but bad news coming from every direction about the global economy, credit markets and the job outlook. Investors were paralyzed with fear as they anticipated even more hits to the stock market on top of the beating they had already taken. In that environment, they withdrew billions of dollars from stock funds and poured that money into bond funds and cash-like securities that they viewed as stable safe harbors.

Do you remember what happened next? Starting in March, 2009, stocks began staging one of their most impressive rallies in history—gaining 178 percent during the next five years. Bonds, meanwhile, didn't return anywhere near that number. Yet, most investors were fearfully fleeing from stocks as fast as they could—right when they should have been investing heavily in them. In fact, they continued to pull money from stock funds during each of the next four years.

Ask yourself how you reacted back in those dark days of 2008 and

2009. Did you think rationally and see that it was a perfect opportunity to buy stocks right before they rallied? Or were you like most investors—nervous, maybe even a bit panicked, and looking for any non-equity investment that you hoped would keep your money safe? Even if you *did* think stocks were a bargain, did you have the courage it took to buy a big buyer of stocks when the outlook seemed dismal?

I can tell you what we did. In late 2008, our firm sent a 12-page letter to our clients outlining the case for one of the greatest buying opportunities in our lifetimes. Suggesting that our clients jump into equities at the depths of the worst market collapse since the Great Depression seemed gutsy to some. However, the history of market overreactions, along with valuations that implied the end of capitalism as we know it, strongly argued for sticking with one's asset allocation and therefore rebalancing back into equities.

4. It's expensive to try to beat the market. Actively managed funds, which tend to shift in and out of stocks and markets and make trades frequently, charge an average expense ratio of 1.5 percent[5]—a cost that is passed on to the investors in those funds. In contrast, many passively managed funds that are designed to capture the return of a particular market or asset class charge much lower expenses—typically around 0.25 percent or even less. When you lower the cost of investing, you boost your bottom line and keep more money in your wallet.

MAXIMIZE YOUR PROBABILITY OF SUCCESS

The goal here is not to present active management strategies as the biggest source of ruin among investors. Rather, the point is to help guide you toward making the types of decisions that will maximize the probability of you achieving the financial goals that are most important to you and your family. The evidence overwhelmingly suggests that the best course of action that you as an investor can take is to let the markets work for you instead of trying to outsmart the markets and end up having them work against you. By focusing your attention on "what works"—capturing the returns that are yours to take—and avoiding the rest, you will put yourself on the right path to a lifetime of investment success.

In the next chapter, you will see how focusing on certain segments of the broad capital markets can enable you to enhance your returns over time by taking only those risks that pay off.

1 "Determinants of Portfolio Performance," 1986. Gary Binson. *Financial Analysts Journal*

2 http://static.cdn-seekingalpha.com/uploads/2013/10/414172_13820471376175_rId12.png

3 http://www.nasdaq.com/article/the-underperformance-culprit-active-management-or-active-managers-cm290665

4 http://www.rhsmith.umd.edu/faculty/rwermers/FDR_published.pdf

5 Motleyfool.com

CHAPTER 6

THE RISK AND RETURN RELATIONSHIP: TAKE ONLY THE INVESTMENT RISKS THAT PAY OFF

WHILE IT'S HARD TO BELIEVE SOMETIMES, markets really **are** efficient over the long-haul. The path to your financial goals is rarely stress-free or non-stop, but countless studies confirm that markets work very well over time. They work even more impressively for disciplined investors who stick to their flight plan and who avoid the temptation to get in or get out quickly, to chase "hot" opportunities or to hide from the latest "doom and gloom" scenario predicted by guests on their favorite business news programs.

While the stocks that make up the various indexes and sectors change all the time, one thing hasn't varied: Investors are rewarded for the amount of risk that they're willing to bear. Experts say risk and reward are "positively correlated," which means they are, in fact, related. Just keep in mind that not all risks are the same, and it's very important that you understand the difference between the various types of risks. Otherwise, you're just gambling with all the wealth you've worked so hard to accumulate over the years. In addition, you'll be convinced that the markets are "rigged" and always working against you.

As we've seen, certain types of risk-taking are ill-advised: trying to pick winning stocks—and thereby avoid the losers; trying to "time" the markets and business cycles; or trying to get into top-rated funds or investments with the "all-star" manager of the moment, to name a few.

However, there's a different type of risk-taking—***smart, calculated, disciplined risk-taking*** that will reward you over the long term.

Over the past 50 years, academic research has identified variables that appear to explain the differences in average returns among stocks. The variables (or premiums) that have stood up to rigorous testing are considered dimensions of expected returns.

ADVANCEMENTS IN RESEARCH

Single-factor (or market factor) model:

During the 1960s, noted economist and professor, William Sharpe and others conducted asset pricing research that led to the development of the Capital Asset Pricing Model (CAPM), which proposed the market as a dimension of expected return. Known also as the single-factor model, CAPM reinforced the value of diversification and provided a simple, rational approach to measuring investment risk and expected returns relative to the market.

Size effect:

Advanced research during the 1970s identified additional factors in stock performance. In 1981, Rolf Banz observed that stocks of companies with small market capitalizations tended to have higher returns than stocks of companies with large market capitalizations. The so-called "size effect" provided a more detailed framework for understanding the dimensions of equity performance.

Value effect:

In a highly influential paper[1] published in 1992, then University of Chicago Professors Eugene Fama and Kenneth French synthesized much of the previous research on asset pricing and found that stocks with low relative prices (or high book-to-market ratios) offered higher average returns than companies with high relative prices (i.e. low book-to-market ratios). They concluded that company size (small vs. large) and relative price (value vs. growth) were strong determinants of stock performance, and when combined with the market, explained most of the average differences among stock returns.

If the name Eugene Fama sounds familiar, that's because he was awarded the Nobel Prize in Economic Science late in 2013.

Figure 6.1 Structure Determines Performance

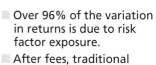 Over 96% of the variation in returns is due to risk factor exposure.

After fees, traditional management typically reduces returns.

4% Stock Picking and Market Timing

The Model Tells the Difference between Investing and Speculating

| average expected return (minus T-bills) | = | average excess return | + | sensitivity to market [market return minus T-bills] | + | sensitivity to size [small stocks minus big stocks] | + | sensitivity to BtM [value stocks minus growth stocks] | + | random error e(t) |

Priced Risk
• Positive expected return
• Systematic
• Economic
• Long-term
• Investing

Unpriced Risk
• Noise
• Random
• Short-term
• Speculating

Source: Dimensional Fund Advisors, 2002 Study.

THE FOUR DIMENSIONS OF RISK THAT COMPENSATE INVESTORS

What does all this research mean to you as an investor? It means that most of the variation in returns among equity portfolios can be explained by the portfolios' relative exposure to three risk factors that have been shown to compensate investors over time:

1. Equity or market risk

Stocks have higher expected returns than fixed income securities, such as U.S. Treasury bills and government bonds. Market risk is the risk you bear for investing your capital anywhere in the stock market—individual companies, industry sectors or market-wide indexes—as opposed to investing in virtually "risk free" assets such as government bonds or Treasury bills. As many of you are experiencing today, the latter do not yield very much, but provide you with a high degree of assurance that you'll get your money back (and maybe earn a tiny bit of interest or appreciation as a bonus).

Sadly, today's nominal yields are so low that the "real" inflation-adjusted yields on safe bonds are close to zero. At the short-end of the maturity stack, the yields are clearly negative. These returns are made worse by the effects of taxes (current or deferred). This brings an interesting question to the fore- Which is the greater risk: (a) market volatility with positive expected returns or (b) a guaranteed loss over time?

Some refer to market risk as a "systematic risk"—something that cannot be minimized or eliminated by diversifying your holdings. There's also something called "**un**systematic risk"—that's the risk of holding a single company or industry group in your portfolio. Numerous research studies have shown that unsystematic risk tends not to reward you over time. As you'll see in the next chapter, this kind of risk should be "diversified away" as much as possible.

Think of systematic risk as a large storm system—every plane that tries to fly through it is likely to encounter turbulence. Because this is not airline-specific, the risk cannot be diversified away.

A real-world example: When 9/11 struck, all airlines' valuations were hurt. Diversification, within the industry, could not eliminate this risk.

Unsystematic risk, however, may be described by the impact of a catastrophic event on a specific airline. The unexpected diversion and loss of Malaysian Airlines Flight MH370 to the South Indian Ocean hurt Malaysian Airlines' outlook and market valuation—to the tune of 40 percent in 2014—while not affecting the industry in general. This risk could have been diversified away by holding a basket of airline stocks.

When United Airlines announced its 2014 results for the first quarter (a $60 million loss) in the face of industry profits, the company's valuation was adversely affected relative to the industry. This risk clearly could be diversified away, again, by holding a variety of airline stocks.

2. Size risk

Research from Fama and French, among others, has shown that historically, stocks with small market capitalizations tend to reward investors over time with better returns than stocks with large market capitalizations. (Market capitalization is calculated by multiplying a company's shares outstanding by the current market price of one share. So a company with 1 million shares outstanding, whose stock trades at $21 per share, would have a market cap of $21 million.)

This is no coincidence. Small-cap stocks tend to be a lot riskier than large-cap stocks because they typically are shares of firms that are younger, less established and more volatile compared to longstanding large companies. In other words, small-cap stocks are less predictable, day-to-day, and less proven than their larger, older peers are. Smaller cap companies tend to have fewer product lines and fewer overseas operations so they're more vulnerable to their home country's economic cycles. Consequently, their earnings are less predictable and the case can be made that a stock price is based on some multiple of what investors are willing to pay for a company's expected future earnings stream. Think IBM versus Tesla (the electric car maker). They're both in the technology sector. Both have strong U.S. operations. Which one has a longer-term track record?

However, the Tesla's of the world have the potential to grow exponentially in a relatively short period of time—or go out of business, be acquired, or suddenly find their main (often only) product "disrupted" by an even younger upstart competitor. Because of these and other risks, Tesla's investors demand a higher relative return on their money than investors in IBM, (or other huge companies such as Procter & Gamble or General Motors).

3. Price risk

Price risk is a third type of compensated risk. Just as stocks are separated into small caps and large caps, they also are categorized by whether they fall into the "growth" category or the "value" category.

Growth stocks are expected to grow faster than the market overall and are sometimes called glamour or go-go stocks. These F-22s of the investment world usually don't pay dividends, as the companies prefer to reinvest retained earnings in capital projects. Technology and biotech companies are examples of growth stocks.

Value stocks are those that tend to trade at a lower price relative to their fundamentals (e.g., dividends, earnings, and sales). Thus, they're considered "undervalued" by rational investors. Common characteristics of such stocks include a high dividend yield, low price-to-book ratio and/or low price-to-earnings ratio. Value stocks tend to have a high book-to-market (BtM) ratio.

BtM is a popular ratio used to find the value of a company by comparing its "book value" (i.e. its' historical cost or accounting value) to its market value (i.e. its market cap). Basically, growth stocks are those with low book values relative to their market values—that is, they have low book-to-market (BtM) ratios. Value stocks are those with high book values relative to their market values—in other words, they have high book-to-market (BtM) ratios.

It turns out that lower-priced "value" (high BtM) stocks have higher expected returns than higher-priced "growth" (low BtM) stocks. Again, this is not an accident. Low-priced value stocks are priced low for a reason: Investors don't like them. Maybe the companies are in financial distress of some sort or have delivered unremarkable results lately. Because of this uncertainty, investors bid the prices of these companies' shares down— which in turn gives those shares their potential for higher returns in the future as the negative situations at these firms improve.

Structuring a portfolio around the risk factors you're "compensated" for can change your priorities in the investment process. The focus shifts from "chasing returns" (through stock picking or market timing) to letting returns come to you (via diversification across multiple asset classes in a portfolio).

The chart below shows what's called a multi-factor approach. **Just as pilots and control towers must consider multiple factors (e.g. weather, air traffic, pilot fatigue and go-around time) before embarking on a flight, investors must consider multiple factors when it comes to managing and leveraging risk**.

Investors receive an average expected return (above T-bills) according to the relative risks they assume in their portfolios. The main factors driving expected returns are (a) **sensitivity to the market**; (b) **sensitivity to small cap stocks** (size factor), and (c) **sensitivity to value stocks** (as measured by book-to-market ratio). Any additional average expected return in the portfolio might be attributed to unpriced risk.

Figure 6.2 Risk and Return are Related

Equity Market (Complete value-weighted universe of stocks.) Stocks have higher expected returns than fixed income.

Company Size (Measured by market capitalization.) Small company stocks have higher expected returns than large company stocks.

Company Price (Measured by ratio of company book value to market equity.) Lower-priced "value" stocks have higher expected returns than higher-priced "growth" stocks.

■ Prior to the model, "products" were classified into rigid and sometimes arbitrary categories.

■ Style boxes allow for crude strategic allocation

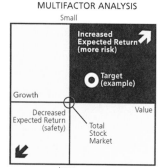

MULTIFACTOR ANALYSIS

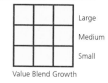

CONSULTING STYLE BOX

Source: Dimensional Fund Advisors

The upshot: The difference in returns among portfolios is largely determined by relative exposure to the market, to small cap stocks, and to value stocks. Stocks offer higher expected returns than fixed income due to the higher perceived risk of being in the market. Many economists further believe that small cap and value stocks outperform large cap and growth because the market "rationally" discounts their prices to reflect their underlying risk. The lower prices give investors greater upside as compensation for bearing this risk.

THE LONG-TERM POWER OF SMALL AND VALUE

Based on the academic research by Dimensional Fund Advisors, there are two types of companies that you might want to weight more heavily than others in your portfolio: **small stocks** and **value stocks**. Focusing on shares of such companies has historically carried acceptable risk because they have long outperformed shares of large companies and growth stocks by remarkable margins. The performance records of these two types of stocks between January of 1926 and December of 2012 is astonishing.

During this period, small stocks outperformed large ones in:

- 622 of 865 rolling 15-year periods,
- 658 of 805 rolling 20-year periods,
- 629 of 685 rolling 30-year periods and
- All 565 of 565 rolling 40-year periods.

During the same period, value stocks (those with depressed prices because they are financially distressed) outperformed growth stocks in:

- 775 of 859 rolling 15-year periods,
- 766 of 799 rolling 20-year periods,
- All 679 of 679 rolling 30-year periods and
- All 559 of 559 rolling 40-year periods.

The reason for this outperformance in the aggregate is the risk premium—investors' reward for taking on more risk. It's just like being a bank. If you are a bank and a small or financially distressed company comes to you for a loan, you're likely to charge the small or financially distressed company more interest than you would charge a large, financially sound company. So, the expected return on these loans should be higher.

The same goes in the stock market. Because risk is perceived to be higher for these companies than for other ones, overall expected returns are higher.

An interesting debate has persisted about whether the small/value premium is solely compensation for risk, or if there's a behavioral component at work. Value companies disproportionately represent the "unloved." Recent academic work, using very sophisticated statistical tools to parse risk from behavior, suggests that this behavioral component is at play.[2] This is significant because, if validated, a value bias pays a return in excess of the return that would be justified solely by a risk premium. In effect, it is a form of free "beta" (excess over market return).

Therefore, investors can do well if, like a judicious loan officer, they manage risk by picking the right companies to invest in. But, as you don't want to take the unacceptable risk of stock-picking, you should buy not a few stocks, ***but potentially hundreds of them***—and there are several efficient ways of doing so. This spreads out risk, positioning you to get the average risk premium of all of these stocks.

The chart below shows the frequency with which the value and size premiums have been positive over various time periods in the U.S. stock market from 1926 to 2012. As the results illustrate, U.S. value stocks have outperformed U.S. growth stocks—and U.S. small cap stocks have outperformed U.S. large cap stocks—in a majority of all the return periods measured. The U.S. value premium has been positive more often than the size premium.

The time periods, which range from five to twenty-five years, are based on annualized returns for rolling 12-month periods (e.g., January-December, February-January, March-February, etc.). The total number of 12-month periods for each time frame is indicated in the footnotes.

Figure 6.3 The Risk Dimensions Delivered

July 1926 – December 2012

OVERLAPPING PERIODS	U.S. Value vs. U.S. Growth	U.S. Small vs. U.S. Large
In 25-Year Periods	Value beat growth 100% of the time.	Small beat large 97% of the time.
In 20-Year Periods	Value beat growth 100% of the time.	Small beat large 88% of the time.
In 15-Year Periods	Value beat growth 95% of the time.	Small beat large 82% of the time.
In 10-Year Periods	Value beat growth 91% of the time.	Small beat large 75% of the time.
In 5-Year Periods	Value beat growth 80% of the time.	Small beat large 60% of the time.

Periods based on rolling annualized returns. 739 total 25-year periods. 799 total 20-year periods. 859 total 15-year periods. 919 total 10-year periods. 979 total 5-year periods. Performance based on Fama/French Research Factors. Securities of small companies are often less liquid than those of large companies. As a result, small company stocks may fluctuate relatively more in price. Mutual funds distributed by DFA Securities LLC.

Source: Dimensional Fund Advisors

EXPECTED PROFITABILITY: A FOURTH DIMENSION

More recently, Fama, French, and other academics have identified expected profitability as a dimension of expected returns.[3] When controlling for size and relative price, research shows that firms that are more profitable have higher expected returns than less profitable firms. Direct profitability appears to offer a robust proxy for this dimension. Direct profitability is a measure of a company's current profits. It is measured as operating income before depreciation and amortization minus interest expense, and then scaled by book equity.

In lay terms, by backing- out "accounting adjustments," we can create a measure of profitability that more closely mirrors real cash income. The evidence suggests that investors can further improve on the value effect by applying this measure to value stocks, which tend to include an above average weighting of distressed companies.

Figure 6.4: The Four Dimensions of Risk that Improve Expected Returns

• Company   ••• Higher Expected Return

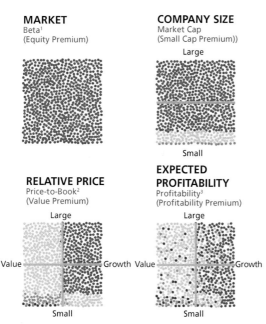

MARKET
Beta[1]
(Equity Premium)

COMPANY SIZE
Market Cap
(Small Cap Premium))
Large
Small

RELATIVE PRICE
Price-to-Book[2]
(Value Premium)
Large
Value Growth
Small

EXPECTED PROFITABILITY
Profitability[3]
(Profitability Premium)
Large
Value Growth
Small

1. Beta: A quantitative measure of the co-movement of a given stock, mutual fund, or portfolio with the overall market.
2. Price-to-Book Ratio: A company't capitalization divided by its book value. It compares the market's valuation of a company to the value of that company as indicated on its financial statements.
3. Profitability: A measure of a company's current profits. We define this as operating income before depreciation and amortization minus interest expense, scaled by book equity.

Source: Dimensional Fund Advisors

BUILDING COMPENSATED RISKS INTO AN OVERALL PORTFOLIO STRATEGY

Financial science has provided a refined, clarifying view of the global equity markets—and investors can apply this knowledge to target dimensions of higher expected return in their portfolios. Investors who want to earn above-market returns must take higher risks in their portfolio. The cross-hair map above illustrates that "tilting" a portfolio toward small cap and value stocks increases the investor's exposure to risk and expected return. Decreasing this exposure relative to the market, results in lower risk and lower expected return.

That said, targeting specific risks should be done within a larger framework of intelligent portfolio construction rather than in isolation. With that in mind, the next chapter will examine the importance of portfolio diversification in the pursuit of both lower volatility and higher returns over the long run.

1 "The Cross-Section of Expected Stock Returns," Eugene F. Fama and Kenneth R. French, *The Journal of Finance*, June 1992

2 "Two Nobel Laureates…Two Tales of Value." Vitali Kalesnik. ResearchAffiliates.com. Nov 2013

3 Fama, Eugene F. and French, Kenneth R., Profitability, Growth, and Average Returns (July 2004). CRSP Working Paper No. 558. Available at SSRN: http://ssrn.com/abstract=570343 or http://dx.doi.org/10.2139/ssrn.570343

CHAPTER 7

DIVERSIFY TO REDUCE VOLATILITY AND BOOST RETURNS

BY NOW, YOU'VE SEEN HOW THE FINANCIAL MARKETS are designed to provide you with positive returns over time. You've also seen that certain segments of the financial markets offer the potential to deliver stronger returns than other segments.

Given those insights, you may be tempted to put all of your investment capital, or the vast majority of it, into those high-flying areas of the financial markets that have shown the most impressive results. If academic research concludes that small-cap and value stocks offer outsized return potential, then why not simply load up on those asset classes, turn on the autopilot and watch your portfolio get bigger and bigger? Indeed, many investors prefer to invest heavily in those areas of the market that they think are poised to generate powerful gains.

Unfortunately, these actions and others like them are a recipe for disappointment. In this chapter, we will examine the risks associated with focusing only on "hot" investments and offer a simple, yet elegant solution: **diversification.**

By building and maintaining a properly diversified portfolio, you will enjoy a smoother investment ride with less volatility and turbulence than you would otherwise experience. This will reduce your stress and increase the confidence that you will achieve your goals. Just as important, a well-diversified portfolio can actually help you earn higher returns and generate more wealth over time.

FROM "WORST TO FIRST," AND BACK: A "TOO-CLOSE-FOR-COMFORT" CASE FOR DIVERSIFICATION

You're probably familiar with the concept of diversification. At the most basic level, diversification means spreading your assets among many different types of investments instead of allocating your money to just one or two. For example, you might diversify your portfolio by owning stocks, bonds and cash. Within your stock holdings, you might own investments from a wide variety of industry sectors (e.g. banking, health care, manufacturing) a variety of company sizes (i.e. large, medium and small), and a variety of investment styles (i.e. growth, value). Within your fixed-income holdings, you might own bonds issued by the government as well as by corporations, and bonds with various maturities.

Some investors view diversification skeptically. Instead of buying a lot of investments that represent the broad spectrum of the financial markets, they ask, why not simply buy a select group of investments that are going to rise in value and outperform all the other asset classes?

There is a very simple reason **not** to do this: *No single company, industry or investment style always performs well.* In fact, it's just the opposite. A strong performing area of the market one year often treads water or loses ground the next; meanwhile, a laggard market segment today comes alive and delivers strong and often unexpected gains tomorrow.

To see this principle in action, consider the following example. Back in 2010, shares of U.S. small-company value stocks[1] topped the performance charts, returning 32.0 percent for the year.[2] The very next year, however, shares of those stocks posted a *negative* 6.1 percent return.[3] Investors who flocked to small-cap value stocks after their impressive 2010 run suffered immediate losses.

Meanwhile, the worst-performing major asset class in 2011 was international value stocks[4]—which plummeted 17.1 percent while other asset classes such as large-cap growth stocks and REITs posted gains.[5] In that environment, most investors would not be highly motivated to own or increase their exposure to the lagging international value segment of the market. However, in 2012, international value stocks soared 21.2 percent—a return that outpaced all other asset classes that year[6].

THE PERILS OF MARKET TIMING

Ah, but couldn't a savvy investor have piled into U.S. small-cap value in early 2010 and then cashed out at just the right moment and avoided the subsequent backslide? While technically possible, remember that the future is by nature unknowable. There's simply no way to be certain that one particular asset class is going to be great or terrible in any given period of time. Indeed, many smart professional investors predicted back in late 2009 that U.S. small-cap value would perform poorly during the coming year. Likewise, in 2012, the general consensus was that international value stocks would continue to suffer. Instead, as noted above, they soared.

This dynamic happens all the time. Think back to 2013. No one—not even the most optimistic bulls on Wall Street—were calling for the broad stock market to rise a robust 30+ percent, which is exactly what happened. On the contrary, many of the loudest market pundits were predicting a down year for stocks in 2013 or a mediocre year at best.

For a "market timing" strategy to work, you have to be someone who is highly adept at knowing exactly when to get in and out of your investments so you can maximize your profits—without leaving money on the table. As we touched on in Chapter 6, the trouble with market timing is that it requires you to get two important decisions right: When to get into an investment (or the market as a whole) and when to get out. While it's possible to make one of these decisions correctly, if you happen to be out of the market on even one of the "big" days of the year, your overall return likely will not match the benchmark indexes and you'll have a portfolio that underperforms, even though you've borne a fair amount of risk.

For example, investors who flee the stock market for the safety of cash may experience temporary relief from market volatility. However, after leaving stocks, their anxiety may shift to concern over missing a stock market rebound while sitting in cash.

The performance data in Figure 7.1 offer one example of the unpredictability of stocks and the hazard of attempting to avoid losses through market timing. The first graph shows returns for the entire first quarter of 2009. The second and third graphs show returns over two distinct periods during that quarter—a negative return period from January 1 to March 9, and a subsequent positive return period from March 10 to the end of the quarter on March 31. The shaded areas in the bars of the third graph indicate the return *excluding* March 10, which marked the first day of the rebound. Although returns for the quarter were negative, the rebound substantially reduced the magnitude of losses.

Figure 7.1: The Perils of Market Timing

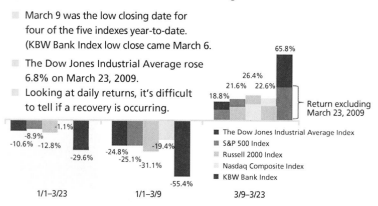

- March 9 was the low closing date for four of the five indexes year-to-date. (KBW Bank Index low close came March 6.
- The Dow Jones Industrial Average rose 6.8% on March 23, 2009.
- Looking at daily returns, it's difficult to tell if a recovery is occurring.

65.8%

26.4%
21.6% 22.6%
18.8%

Return excluding March 23, 2009

-1.1%
-8.9%
-10.6% -12.8%
-29.6%
-24.8%
-25.1%
-31.1%
-19.4%
-55.4%

1/1–3/23   1/1–3/9   3/9–3/23

■ The Dow Jones Industrial Average Index
■ S&P 500 Index
  Russell 2000 Index
  Nasdaq Composite Index
■ KBW Bank Index

Source: Dimensional Fund Advisors

This is the nature of stock investing. Gains often come in powerful upsurges against a backdrop of discouraging financial and economic news. As the March 2009 rally demonstrated, a surprise rebound may frustrate investors who are waiting for an "all clear" signal that it's okay to return to the market. Of course, a brief period like the one above may not signal the start of a new bull market. However, recent history does serve as a reminder of how suddenly a major turnaround can begin.

Your job is to make smart financial decisions, not to try to predict bull and bear markets. You want to be positioned to capture positive performance when it occurs, which is best achieved by holding a broadly diversified portfolio. If your goal is always to own investments that are "winning," you need to own a lot of different assets all the time. Doing so virtually guarantees that your portfolio will have exposure to those segments of the market that are leading the pack during any particular day, week, month or year.

That said, diversification also means that you'll be invested in some areas of the market that aren't performing especially well at any given moment. That's the "cost" of diversification. However, that cost is much lower than the cost of placing a big bet on one or two market segments and getting it wrong. Remember, the financial markets and the entire capitalist system are designed to generate long-term wealth as the majority of companies create value. "Placing a bet" on capitalism by diversifying and owning the entire market is as close to a sure thing as there is. It's just like flying: You want an optimal weight (asset) distribution to ensure a safe, efficient and, hopefully, smooth ride.

MORE WEALTH—WITH LESS STRESS

Because each asset class has a habit of performing well for a while and then performing poorly—and because we can't know with certainty when each asset class will rise or fall—we need to own a lot of different asset classes. That way, gains in your portfolio from asset classes that are doing well can help to offset losses that occur due to poor performance from asset classes that are suffering.

The end result is that you have less fluctuation in the value of your portfolio. Notice I did not say *no fluctuation* in your portfolio's value. Even a well-diversified portfolio will rise and fall and can lose money in a given year. But the swings, both positive and negative, won't be as extreme as they would be if you only owned a small number of asset classes. This "smoother flight" can go a long way toward reducing the stress that many pilots feel when managing their money. If an asset class in your portfolio does poorly, you can breathe a little easier knowing that you have plenty of others that are doing well on a relative or absolute basis. In addition, you'll be less likely to get nervous or panic during extreme periods of market volatility when the headlines are predicting doom.

However, diversification does more than just minimize portfolio volatility and provide greater levels of comfort and confidence. Believe it or not, a well-diversified portfolio can also deliver higher returns than a less-diversified, more volatile portfolio. To put it another way, diversification can bring you more wealth than you would have otherwise. This is because a well-diversified portfolio will minimize "variance drain." Two portfolios with the identical long-term average return, but one more volatile than the other, will result in two different end values. This is not an intuitive concept. The end value of a portfolio is a result of the geometric average return for the time period in question. That portfolio with greater volatility will have a lower *geometric* average return despite the same *arithmetic* average return. The lesson to be learned is that volatility drags down returns, all other factors held equal.

To see how this works, consider **Figure 7.2**, which shows two hypothetical $100,000 portfolios. Each one has the same arithmetic average return over a two-year period—0 percent. But note that portfolio #1 is much more volatile: Its returns ranged from +50 percent to -50 percent, while portfolio #2's returns only swung from +10 percent to -10 percent. As a result of that extra volatility, portfolio #1's *geometric* return was much lower than portfolio #2's. An investor in volatile portfolio #1 would have ended up with much less wealth at the end of the two-year period—$24,000 less, to be exact. In stark contrast, an investor in the less volatile portfolio #2 would have done a much better job protecting wealth. Extrapolate this example over 10, 20 or 30 years and you can start to see how important a diversified, lower-volatility portfolio can be when it comes your bottom line.

Figure 7.2: The Impact of Volatility on a Hypothetical $100,000 Portfolio

	Year 1 Return	Year 2 Return	Average Return	Compound Return	Value at End of Year 2
Portfolio #1	50%	-50%	0%	-13.40%	$75,000
Portfolio #2	10%	-10%	0%	-0.50%	$99,000

DIVERSIFY INTELLIGENTLY

Clearly, diversification offers tremendous benefits. However, it's important to understand that truly effective diversification—the type that provides the potential for lower portfolio volatility and higher geometric portfolio returns—does not necessarily mean simply owning a lot of different stocks or funds.

For example, say you owned 10 mutual funds—all of which invested in shares of large U.S. companies. Such a portfolio cannot be considered to be effectively diversified, because all of the funds invest in the same market segment. When U.S. large-cap stocks rise as a group, all 10 funds can be expected to follow suit. Likewise, when those stocks fall, all 10 funds are likely to suffer losses.

Instead, the key is to own asset classes that don't move in lockstep with each other. That way, when one of your investments is falling in value, another will be rising.

How might an intelligently diversified portfolio be structured? Consider the following guidelines:

1. Own large-caps and small caps. While small-caps have outper-formed large-caps over time (as seen in Chapter 6), there have been multiple periods—some lasting many years—when large-caps have beaten their smaller peers by significant margins. To minimize volatil-ity and maximize wealth, it makes sense to own shares of both types of companies consistently.

The simplest way to own both large- and small-cap equities is to buy a solid, low-cost total market index fund (or ETF). However, traditional index funds substantially overweight large cap and growth funds. A number of alternatives now exist that incorporate the strengths and efficiencies of traditional index funds, but that seek to eliminate the large growth bias. Dimensional Fund Advisors has done a great deal to advance the implementation of Fama and French's research here.

2. Own growth and value. Likewise, growth and value stocks tend to take turns at the controls, and each has gone on extended winning streaks at the expense of the other over time. As noted previously, a bias to value offers improved expected returns.

3. Own domestic and international. Many investors don't realize that non-U.S.-based companies make up approximately 50 percent of the global stock market's capitalization. In other words, you can gain access to roughly half of the world's investment opportunities by owning foreign stocks. Those opportunities include huge players in their industries (such as BP and Novartis) as well as smaller outfits that are highly successful in their home countries (even if they're not household names in the U.S.). Many international markets tend to perform well when the U.S. market is down, and vice versa.

Often overlooked is the fact that the largest U.S. multinationals are just that: multinational. Therefore, a domestic large-cap index fund will have some international exposure. Additional diversification and rebalancing value can be gained by adding international assets (both developed and emerging markets) to the mix.

4. Own short-term, high-quality bonds. Most investors know that bonds maintain their value or even rise when stocks fall. That fact alone makes bonds an important part of a diversified portfolio. That said, one category of bonds—high-quality, short-term bonds—is the best for achieving truly effective diversification. The reason, once again, comes back to taking risks that actually pay off.

Long-term bonds of lower quality are significantly more volatile than short-term, high-quality issues. However they don't offer much in the way of additional returns. In other words, long-term lower-quality bonds don't give you adequate compensation for the amount of risk you incur by owning them. For effective diversification benefits, stick with high-quality short-term bonds that offer lower volatility and values that are more stable.

A KEY COMPONENT IN YOUR SUCCESS

Ultimately, diversification is one of your biggest allies in your flight plan for wealth. Not only does it help you avoid taking risks that come with potentially enormous costs, it also positions your wealth to grow faster than it would otherwise.

Once you know that you want to diversify your portfolio and how you want to diversify, it's time to set out and actually build a well-diversified portfolio using specific investment vehicles. In the next chapter, we'll explore the best options for creating a superior portfolio.

1 As measured by the DFA U.S. Small Cap Index

2 BAM Advisor Services (http://www.bamadvisorservices.com/img/CanYouPickNextWinner.jpg)

3 BAM Advisor Services (http://www.bamadvisorservices.com/img/CanYouPickNextWinner.jpg)

4 As measured by the F/F International Value Index

5 BAM Advisor Services (http://www.bamadvisorservices.com/img/CanYouPickNextWinner.jpg)

6 BAM Advisor Services (http://www.bamadvisorservices.com/img/CanYouPickNextWinner.jpg)

CHAPTER 8

PORTFOLIO CONSTRUCTION STRATEGIES

BY NOW, YOU'VE SEEN HOW THE FINANCIAL MARKETS are designed to provide you with positive returns over time. You've also seen that certain segments of the financial markets offer the potential to deliver stronger returns than other segments. We've also seen how to diversify your holdings to reduce volatility and boost returns.

As we mentioned in our previous chapter, diversification is one of your biggest allies in your flight plan for wealth. Not only does it help you avoid taking risks that come with potentially enormous costs; it also positions your wealth to grow faster than it would otherwise.

Here, we'll explore the best options for creating a superior portfolio that's tailored to your life goals, your time horizon and your risk tolerance. Now you understand that you need to own a broadly diversified mix of asset classes to build a superior portfolio. What is the best way to own (and take advantage of) asset classes? The ideal way is through asset class funds that enable you to capture the returns of each asset class you wish to own—and do so in the most tax- and cost-effective manner.

ASSET CLASS INVESTING

The decision about which asset classes to own is what drives the overwhelming portion of return within a portfolio (stocks vs. bonds, international vs. domestic, small vs. large, value vs. growth). Failing to focus a portfolio on the asset classes that are most appropriate for each individual investor's unique circumstances is a common mistake made by novice investors, as well as by seasoned professional managers.

Most portfolio managers focus on activities that ultimately mean very little in the long run— trying to pick the "right" stocks and exactly the right time to buy or sell them. As a result, the most critical elements of the portfolio's return are often neglected. In addition, "active" managers tend to charge high fees, and also increase taxes and transaction costs as a result of frequent trading.

To get around this, many investors (and advisors) turn to large fund companies to replicate commercial indexes (such as the S&P 500, Russell 2000, MSCI, and others) in order to provide low-cost returns of certain asset classes. While indexing is low in cost and generates returns that are *close* to the indexes they mirror, this strategy can fall short for several reasons:

1. Replication of indexes generates inefficiencies of trading index-identified stocks on specific days along with other index funds. This competition to buy and sell is a cost to the index that reduces returns.

2. Commercial indexes are merely a "description" of an asset class. That description rarely, if ever, contains the dimensions of the asset class that are the most attractive to an investor historically. For example, while the Russell 2000 Value is used to describe small cap value, research shows that you can get more attractive exposure to the asset class by owning *smaller* and more *"valuey"* stocks than the index. Again, this decision on portfolio structure (how to best get small cap value exposure) explains the returns.

As mentioned earlier, index funds carefully track commercial indexes such as the S&P 500 to help investors "buy the market." Asset class investors try to capture the returns of the same asset classes. However, because asset class investing doesn't promise to follow a particular index *slavishly*, it doesn't have to own precisely the same securities (or the same number of securities) in those indexes at the same times.

This comes in handy when new companies come into the indexes and index funds must buy them, no matter what their (inflated) prices are. Savvy asset class investors will try to wait to buy these securities when they are cheaper. The hot IPO of the moment, for instance, won't turn up in their funds for a while either, since research from DFA[1] among others, shows that stocks of IPOs generally underperform the market early in their existence.

INDEX INVESTING VS. ASSET CLASS INVESTING

Many investors might believe that passive investing means simply buying index funds. However, there are some key differences between index investing and passive asset class investing. Let's look closer at some of those differences.

Many investors realize that a passive investment approach offers numerous benefits over an active investment approach. Passive investing involves buying and holding market *components*, whereas an active investor or fund manager tries to pick the next winning stock (or time) where the market is headed next. A passive approach offers these major benefits:

- By holding entire market components, one maximizes the benefits of diversification.

- By "tilting" the portfolio to riskier or less risky components, the investor can expect to capture the highest market return given his or her risk tolerance.

- The investor maintains control over his or her own portfolio's components (by avoiding active funds' tendency to style drift without the investor's knowledge).

- Expenses can be minimized.
- Tax efficiency can be maximized.

To implement a passive investment approach, investors can choose from:

- Index mutual funds
- Exchange-traded funds (ETFs), and
- Passively managed asset class funds

Investors may wonder, "Why shouldn't I just buy index funds instead of passively managed asset class funds? What is the benefit of passive asset class management versus 'index' investing?"

The historical evidence[2] has shown that index investing and passive asset class investing are superior strategies to investing in individual stocks or actively managed mutual funds. However, building a portfolio of passive asset class funds expands upon the benefits of index investing while minimizing some of its potential negatives.

First, let's explore the differences between the two. *All index funds are passively managed, but not all passive asset class funds are index funds.* An asset class is a group of stocks with similar risk characteristics, such as domestic or international, large-cap or small-cap. An asset class also can be a combination of similar risk characteristics, such as "U.S. small-cap value stocks" or "international large-cap growth stocks." An investment firm can create its own definition of an asset class and then passively manage a fund based on that definition. *In such cases, there may not always be a specific index that represents or tracks that asset class.*

Passive asset class funds retain the benefits of indexing. They are relatively low cost, low turnover and tax efficient. However, they improve on the index model through additional strategies. Let's look at some of the ways a passive asset class fund can improve returns.

HOW ETS'S FIT INTO THE ASSET CLASS MODEL

Exchange Traded Funds (ETFs)

Exchange-Traded Funds (ETF) are investment funds traded on stock exchanges, much like stocks. An ETF holds assets such as stocks, commodities, or bonds, and trades close to its net asset value over the course of the trading day. Most ETFs track an index, such as a stock index or bond index. ETFs may be attractive as investments because of their low costs, tax efficiency, and stock-like features.

How ETFs differ from mutual funds and index funds

ETFs offer investors an undivided interest in a pool of securities and other assets and, thus, are similar in many ways to traditional mutual funds, except that shares in an ETF can be bought and sold throughout the day on a stock exchange. ETFs have several similarities to mutual funds. Like a mutual fund, an ETF is a pool or basket of investments. An ETF may have lower transaction and/or operating expenses than its' equivalent passive fund, assuming one exists. In this case, we would recommend the ETF. However, an ETFs construction and implementation may result in less advantage than appears at first glance.

Another primary difference is that an ETF doesn't trade at the end of the day the way a mutual fund does. The price of the ETF is determined by investor demand at any given time during the trading day.

ETF tax efficiency

ETFs can be more tax efficient than mutual funds. Unlike mutual-funds in which shares are redeemed with the fund directly, ETFs are traded on an exchange just like a stock is. When one party sells the ETF and another buys it on the exchange, the underlying securities within the ETF are not sold to raise cash for the redemption, therefore no gain/ no tax. This advantage is minimal when comparing a passive ETF with a passive fund.

CREATING BUY-AND-HOLD RANGES

Index funds must sell a stock when it leaves the index. For example, if a small-cap stock increases in market capitalization so that it is no longer part of the small cap index, the fund tracking that index is required to sell it. This creates turnover and tax inefficiency.

By contrast, a passive asset class fund has the flexibility to create buy-and-hold ranges that enable the fund to hold a stock even if it falls out of the appropriate index. When properly implemented, buy-and-hold ranges help reduce turnover and increase tax efficiency while still enabling the fund to remain true to its stated asset class definitions. For example, a passive asset class small cap fund might establish a range in which it *buys* all stocks in the smallest 8 percent of market cap. But the same fund might establish a rule that it won't *sell* the stock unless it grows beyond the smallest 10 percent.

MANAGING TRACKING ERROR

Tracking error (also known as "active risk") is a measure of how closely a portfolio follows the index to which it is benchmarked. The lower the tracking error, the more closely the fund follows its benchmark index.

Index funds can't really have tracking error—they must look exactly like the index that they're replicating. However, asset class funds **can** have tracking error, and under some circumstances, tracking error can be a good thing because it means lower turnover (lower costs to shareholders) and better tax efficiency. It can also mean the fund was not required to buy into rapidly falling stocks, just to replicate the index, which can result in positive "outperformance."

However, in a bull market, the advisor and investment managers have some explaining to do when track error occurs. Having deep relationships with our clients enables us to invest the time explaining to clients why the tracking error they see actually improves their portfolio's efficiency. Tracking error also comes into play with respect to dividend management. We'll discuss that later in this chapter.

ELIMINATING CERTAIN STOCK TYPES

Based upon academic evidence, some stock types have been demonstrated to result in historically poor returns, and passive asset class funds can screen these stocks. For example, initial public offering (IPO) stocks have demonstrated poor historical returns in the initial years following their IPO. Based on this evidence, a passive asset class fund might eliminate all IPO stocks until they have seasoned a certain number of years, at which point they become eligible for purchase.

Listing requirements for NASDAQ stocks are much less stringent than those for New York Stock Exchange stocks. As a result, far more NASDAQ stocks are eventually "delisted" due to fraud and other financial weaknesses. By establishing a screen calling for greater financial requirements (such as those of the National Market System), a passive fund can reduce its exposure to stocks that eventually delist.

ESTABLISHING ADDITIONAL COMMON-SENSE SCREENS

Passive asset class funds are essentially free to establish additional screens that can be demonstrated to improve net returns. For example, the trading costs for small cap stocks can be significantly higher than those for large cap stocks. Why? Because small cap stocks typically experience lower levels of liquidity. Therefore, a passive fund might establish a screen so that no stock will be traded unless there are a certain minimum number of "market makers" (i.e., parties interested in trading the stock).

TAKING ADVANTAGE OF BLOCK TRADING TECHNIQUES

A small cap passive asset class fund can also take advantage of its ability to remain flexible regarding its precise market cap weighting, whereas an index fund generally must maintain its specific defined weighting. By acting as a market maker in small cap stocks, the passive asset class fund can earn not only the bid-offer spread, but it can also earn market effect costs.

The preceding terminology can be daunting even to relatively sophisticated investors. Hopefully this example will help: Suppose an actively managed fund is selling a large block of a small cap stock that is trading at 10 bid-10.5 asked (which means the broker/dealer is willing to buy at 10 and sell at 10.5). The stock has typically been trading just 30,000 shares per day, but the active fund wants to immediately sell 100,000 shares. However, selling such a large number of shares relative to the stock's typical trading level will drive the price much lower—even before they are done selling.

Before moving on with our illustration, it is important to understand that the stock's next move is random, as proven by EMH. The fact that an active fund manager is attempting to sell a stock does not actually indicate whether the stock will move up or down. Therefore, a passive fund can benefit from what is more than likely a misplaced sense of urgency on the part of the active manager. For example, a passive asset class fund might establish a range of appropriate market cap weightings it is willing to own — such as ranging from half to double its target holding.

Returning to our illustration, the passive asset class fund manager might check the fund's current holdings, determine it is holding 200,000 shares and conclude that it can hold up to 400,000, given the range it has established. Knowing that he or she can purchase the 100,000 shares and that the active fund is desperate to sell, the passive fund manager might submit a bid of 9.5. If the bid is won, the likelihood is that the stock will return to trading at 10 bid-10.5 asked. The passive fund might then offer a small amount of stock at 10.375. It may even find a buyer who is looking to buy a large block and pay a premium for it. By earning the bid-ask spread and the market impact cost, the passive asset class fund has created the potential to enhance returns through negative trading costs.

ADDING TAX MANAGEMENT STRATEGIES

As we have seen, passive asset class funds have many advantages over index funds. However, passively managed funds that also engage in tax management strategies can do even better.

While passive asset class funds are already relatively tax efficient (compared with actively managed funds), there are additional strategies that can be employed to further improve their after-tax returns. These strategies include the following techniques:

- Fund managers can avoid taking intentional short-term capital gains. Stocks that should be sold because they have moved beyond their hold ranges are not sold if they are not yet eligible for long-term capital gains treatment. Once the required one-year holding period is reached, the stocks will then be sold. This lowers the tax rate on the capital gain from ordinary income tax rates to the lower long-term capital gains rate.

- Stocks that have significant losses can be sold to harvest those losses. The stocks can then be repurchased following the 30-day waiting period required to avoid violating the wash sale rule.

- Specific lot accounting is used to minimize realized gains on sale. The stocks sold have the highest cost basis.

- Fund managers can avoid purchasing stocks just prior to the ex-dividend date. This reduces the amount of income that will be taxed at higher ordinary income tax rates.

ADDING DIVIDEND MANAGEMENT

By focusing on minimizing dividends, fund managers can expect to improve upon after-tax returns. The Fama-French three-factor model tells us that almost all of the variance of equity portfolio returns can be explained by exposure to the risk factors of size (market cap) and value. Thus, two portfolios with similar market caps and similar book-to-market ratios have similar expected returns.

According to the same model, dividends are *not* a factor in expected returns. A fund that seeks to minimize dividend income can screen for stocks with high dividends, yet it can still own a portfolio with sensitivities to the small cap and value factors that are very similar to a portfolio that includes the high-dividend-paying stocks. As such, the fund can enjoy the same expected pretax returns. The portfolio can be targeted to provide just enough yield to offset the fund's expense ratio, which can result in no net dividend income (and resulting tax burden) to shareholders.

Note that investors who take advantage of funds that implement dividend management must be aware of (and prepared to tolerate) "tracking error" which we discussed earlier in this chapter. A fund that manages dividends has the same expected pretax returns as a fund that does not. However, that fund will hold a significantly different portfolio in terms of specific stocks, so its returns can (and often do) deviate substantially from its relative benchmark. The tracking error should be random and thus short-term in nature. But, when it does occur, investors must be prepared to stay the course and ignore it, rather than panic and feel the approach is not working.

OTHER ADVANCED INVESTMENT TECHNIQUES

Research from DFA, among others, has provided investors with a road map to a prudent investment strategy that is based on passive investing. Building a globally diversified portfolio of passive asset class funds is most likely to allow all levels of investors to achieve their financial goals with the least amount of risk, particularly when they partner with an investment advisor who is experienced at implementing and maintaining a passive asset class portfolio.

Once a portfolio has been constructed, it needs to be integrated into the client's household and implemented so that it maximizes the portfolio's potential and captures efficiencies specific to the client's accounts. These efficiencies, in aggregate, account for a substantial spread in the relative performance over the same portfolio that is "blindly" managed.

ASSET LOCATION AND TAX EFFICIENCY

Once you've determined the specific types of asset class funds that you want to use to implement your portfolio strategy, you need to determine which types of accounts are best suited for each fund. This is where the concept of asset location comes into play. Asset location is about determining which securities should be held in tax-deferred accounts and which securities should be held in taxable accounts in order to maximize after-tax returns.

The generic asset allocation process is normally implemented at the account level. The net effect is that three different accounts could have three identical allocations regardless of their size and/or their tax status.

Asset location is the process of taking an asset allocation and assigning different asset classes to specific accounts based on (a) the tax footprint of the underlying investments and (b) the tax treatment of each individual account.

HOW ASSET LOCATION MINIMIZES TAXES

A typical investor with a balanced portfolio consisting of 60 percent stocks and 40 percent bonds might hold investments in both taxable accounts and tax-deferred accounts. Although the investor's overall portfolio should be balanced, each account does not need to have the same asset mix. Creating the same asset allocation in each account ignores the tax benefit of placing securities properly in the type of account that will assure the best after-tax return.

The way in which a security is taxed will determine where it should be *located*. Dividends and capital gains get favorable treatment. While interest income gets taxed as normal income (39.6 percent rate for investors in the highest tax bracket), the tax rate for dividends and capital gains is only 23.8 percent (including 3.8 percent for the Affordable Care Act). Since most equity investments generate returns from both dividends and capital gains, investors realize lower tax bills when holding stocks or equity mutual funds within a taxable account. Those same capital gains and dividends, however, would be taxed at the ordinary rate (up to 39.6 percent) if withdrawn from a traditional IRA, 401(k), 403(b), or other type of retirement account where taxes are paid on the withdrawal of funds.

Fixed-income investments, such as bonds and real estate investment trusts (REITs) generate a regular cash flow. These interest payments are subject to the same ordinary income tax rates of up to 39.6

percent. A tax-deferred retirement account provides investors with a shelter for this income.

For example, real estate investment trusts (REITs) are required to pay out at least 90 percent of their income each year and that income is usually treated as ordinary income. In other words, that income must be taxed at the investor's top marginal rate, so REITS have an awful tax footprint. By using asset location techniques, we seek to limit REIT exposure to an IRA or to other ordinary-income tax deferred accounts. With asset location, we make this type of decision for every asset class as needed, given the client's unique financial and tax situation.

The asset location process also results in fewer transactions for the client's portfolio, hence, lower costs. That's because the rebalancing process is not conducted at the account level, but at the household or client level.

ACHIEVING OPTIMAL ASSET LOCATION

While asset location can result in lower taxes for an investor, it is not a replacement for *asset allocation*. Only after you determine the proper asset mix for your portfolio can you then locate those investments in the appropriate accounts to minimize the tax drag on your investments. The best location for an investor's assets depends on a number of different factors including financial profile, prevailing tax laws, investment holding periods, and the tax and return characteristics of the underlying securities. However, there are some general principles for the types of investments that are best-suited to each type of account.

Tax harvesting opportunities, **which we'll talk more about in the next chapter,** are evaluated on an annual basis: Toward the end of each year we review our client's taxable accounts for any asset showing a possible capital loss. If we can harvest the loss for a write-off, we will replace the asset in question. Alternatively, should the client have substantial tax loss carry-forwards, we may decide to harvest a gain and offset it against a carry-forward. These activities are collectively known as tax harvesting, and can add real value in terms of after-tax (real net) returns.

At Efficient Wealth Management, we have developed a range of models (asset allocations) that are designed to take advantage of the full body of research available. Because we are more interested in risk-adjusted "purity" and in harvesting known anomalies, our models tend to trend closer to those developed by DFA. We prefer DFA's models to the more generic models built for retail use.

TACTICAL ASSET ALLOCATION AND CAPTURING PERSISTENT ANOMALIES

At Efficient Wealth Management, the design and construction of our portfolios is constantly reevaluated to take advantage of relative market weightings of different asset classes. Though we don't try to time the market, we do take advantage of self-evident swings in relative valuation between asset classes. This is known as dynamic asset allocation.

We also design our portfolios to capture the well documented value premium and small cap premiums that persist over time. Again, as renowned economists Eugene Fama and Kenneth French discovered over long periods of time, stocks with high price to book value ratios (i.e. value stocks) tend to outperform growth stocks and stocks with relatively small market capitalizations tend to outperform stocks with large market capitalizations over long periods of time.[3]

In addition, we recommend diversifying among a wide range of asset classes with a view to maximizing the potential efficiency of the portfolio for any given risk tolerance. For instance, one of the goals of a well-designed portfolio is to minimize "Variance Drain." This is the phenomenon in which two portfolios with the identical long-term *average* returns, will result in two differing end values. Why? Because one portfolio is a lot more volatile than the other. *See Figure 7-2 in previous chapter for more.*

As we discussed in the previous chapter, variance drain is not an intuitive concept. The end value of a portfolio is a result of the geometric average return for the time period in question. The portfolio with greater volatility will have a lower geometric average despite the same arithmetic average return. **The lesson to be learned is that volatility drags down returns**, all other factors being equal. One of the objectives of a portfolio that is efficiently rebalanced is to reduce the volatility of that portfolio and hence earn a greater risk-adjusted return and reduce trading costs.

PORTFOLIO EFFICIENCY (MANAGING THE COSTS)

At the end of the day, you want to put as much of your hard-earned wealth to work for you as possible. That's why it's so important to keep the costs of all of your investing activities as low as possible in order to meet your objectives.

For a $1 million portfolio, each percentage point in annual expenses is equivalent to $10,000 that's not put to work for you. Compound that $10,000 every year by a historical 8 percent annual rate of return and you can see it adds up to tens of thousands, if not hundreds of thousands of dollars, in foregone return.

Figure 8.1 High Costs make Outperformance Difficult—The Winners and Losers based on Expense Ratios

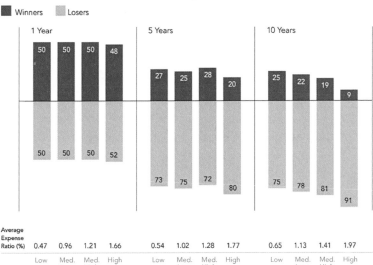

Source: Dimensional Fund Advisors. "Mutual Fund Landscape Report 2014"

Most retail investors are unaware of the range and volume of expenses that drag down their investment performance. Some expenses are obvious (e.g. advisory fees, commissions, front-end loads, management fees and transaction costs). Some of the fees are not so obvious, such are expenses related to "bid-ask spreads'", 12b-1 fees, short-term versus long-term capital gains and wrap fees. Put together, these expenses typically add about 2.5 percent to the cost structure of the portfolio—that's $25,000 a year on a $1 million portfolio.

Hybrid investments such as annuities, hedge funds, structured investments and other broker-sold offerings often have cost structures ranging from 5 percent to 8 percent or more! The markets are not perfectly efficient; but they're efficient enough. There's no evidence that these more sophisticated investments justify their enormous costs. However, they're widely and aggressively sold and for good reason: The commissions are fabulous for brokers and financial services providers who sell them.

A core premise of Efficient Wealth Management is to apply relentless efficiency to the development and implementation of our clients' portfolios. When all other factors are equal, we select on the basis of cost. We accept no commissions, no kick-backs, no "soft-dollars" or other incentives—and we state so clearly and publicly in our regulatory filings (our ADV) so that we are held to that standard by our regulators.

Costs count. After the asset allocation, the next most important determinant of portfolio performance is the underlying cost structure of that portfolio. Remarkably, though the average total expense drag on mutual funds exceeds 2 percent, we often have large portions of the client's portfolio invested in vehicles with expense ratios as low as 0.15 percent or, in some cases, even less. These cost savings are, in effect, improved returns free of additional risk.

Depending on the asset class, the flexibility to reduce costs varies somewhat, but Efficient is our first name. Efficient Wealth Management seeks to use cost efficient index and exchange traded funds whenever possible and when the cost advantage is not outweighed by some offsetting fact (which is very rare, in practice). It is our stated objective to reduce the client's existing cost structure by more than enough to pay our management fees, thereby, enabling the client to enjoy our wealth management suite of services for little or no net cost.

Now you know how to build a portfolio, which types of assets and funds to use and where to put them for maximum tax efficiency and cost efficiency. In the next chapter, we'll explore the art and science of monitoring and rebalancing your portfolio.

1 Frick, Bob. "This Is Rocket Science." Kiplinger's Personal Finance Oct. 2008. Kiplinger Personal Finance Archive. Web. http://www.kiplinger.com/magazine/archives/2008/10/DFA_funds.html?kipad_id=x

2 Sharpe, William F. "The Arithmetic of Active Management" *The Financial Analysts' Journal* January/February 1991 http://web.stanford.edu/~wfsharpe/art/active/active.htm

3 Fama, Eugene; French Kenneth "Common Risk Factors in the Returns on Stocks and Bonds" *Journal of Financial Economics,* February 1993

CHAPTER 9

STAYING ON COURSE: THE NEED TO MONITOR AND REBALANCE

YOUR JOB IS NOT DONE once you've assembled a portfolio of investments that reflect your objectives. You need to monitor how those investments are performing and how effective they are at getting you to your carefully defined goals. You also must determine if you need to make any adjustments to your portfolio based on any changes you've experienced in your life lately or recent developments that have occurred in the financial markets.

STAYING COMMITTED TO YOUR STRATEGY

Once you develop and implement a portfolio of investments that are designed around your specific goals and objectives, you need to maintain that strategy in order for it to work as it should and deliver the returns you expect to generate.

If, instead, you change your allocation frequently by shifting in and out of various asset classes and investments, you can easily jeopardize your financial future.

To see just how important it is to stay on track with your plan, consider the chart below. It shows the performance of the S&P 500 from 1994 to 2013. Over that entire twenty-year period, the index returned 9.22 percent annually. If you owned an asset class fund that performed roughly in line with that index over the entire period, you would have enjoyed a similar return.

However, let's say you often moved your money around during that time—perhaps selling some or all of your stocks whenever the headlines made you nervous about the equity market and loading up on bonds to get some "safety," then repeated the process. Chances are, all that jumping around would have cost you plenty. As you can see, if you missed just the best 10 days for the index during that entire period, your return would have dropped to just 5.49 percent. *Miss the best 40 days and you actually would have lost money on your investment!*

The Problem with Market Timing: Missing the Best Days
20 Years (1/1/1994 - 12/31/2013)

$10,000 Invested in the S&P 500 Index	S&P 500 Annualized Return	Value of $10,000 at the end of the period	Gain/ Loss	Impact of Missing Days
All 5,037 trading days	9.22%	$58,352	$48,352	--
Less the 5 days with the biggest gains	7.00%	$38,710	$28,710	-40.62%
Less the 10 days with the biggest gains	5.49%	$29,121	$19,121	-60.45%
Less the 20 days with the biggest gains	3.02%	$18,146	$8,146	-83.15%
Less the 40 days with the biggest gains	-1.02%	$8,149	-$1,851	-103.83%

© 2014 Index Fund Advisors, Inc. (IFA.com)   Source: Yahoo! Finance - Created: 1/7/14

Clearly, a lot of the returns you can get from your equity investments will occur on just a handful of days. If you're not in the market to capture those returns, you will miss out—and potentially end up with a lot less wealth for yourself and your family.

That said, it can be difficult to maintain your strategy and stick to your plan during periods when some asset classes are performing poorly. For example, it's likely that you were tempted to sell stocks back in 2008 when U.S. equities were falling by more than 30 percent. Likewise, it's tempting to load up on "hot" asset classes that have performed well in recent months or years. Unfortunately, that decision typically leads to losses when those hot investments suddenly cool off—and your realize that you got on the runway too late or simply stayed on the tarmac too long

THE VALUE OF THE INVESTMENT POLICY STATEMENT

Fortunately, there are ways to help you maintain your flight plan over the long run and avoid making rash moves with your wealth that could take you off course.

One of the most important tools is an investment policy statement (IPS). An IPS is a written document that spells out in detail the rules for the implementation of your portfolio strategy.

Those rules reflect the key considerations discussed so far in this book—including your goals, needs, risk tolerance, time horizon and investment preferences. By putting all that information down in writing into a formal document, you gain much needed clarity about what you are investing for and why you are investing the way you are. By knowing the "what" and the "why"—and by having a written document available to remind you about those things at any time—you will be able to maintain your long-term plan for your wealth better regardless of what the markets throw your way in the short term.

A good IPS also should include the disbursement policy to be adopted once you retire. At our firm, we have developed a methodology designed to give clients a statistically measurable level of confidence that they will never outlive their portfolio despite the variability of markets, the need for inflation adjustments and the provision of taxes. This is a complex but important decision that has irrevocably negative outcomes if mishandled. Disbursement policies will be discussed in more detail in the next chapter.

THE IMPORTANCE OF REVIEWING YOUR WEALTH MANAGEMENT PLAN

It's also important to regularly review your financial goals and the amount of progress your wealth management plan is making toward achieving them. The process of monitoring and reviewing will help you see if you are still on track to achieve your objectives on your timetable—or if you need to make any changes to your plan that will help you maximize your probability of a successful outcome.

Every quarter, it makes good sense to sit down and review your plan. This process involves three steps:

1. Identify any changes in your life—personal, professional or financial—that could impact your Wealth Management plan.
Take a few minutes to think about any major new occurrences in your life in recent months, or any that are coming down the road. A birth, a death, a new career, a divorce, a job loss, or an unexpected inheritance—significant events such as these and others can have a sizable effect on your immediate financial needs as well as your future financial goals. They also might raise or lower the amount of risk you can comfortably take with your investments. For example, it could be prudent to reduce your exposure to risky assets temporarily if you suffer a job loss and need access to cash.

2. Assess your portfolio's performance. Remember that your portfolio will almost certainly consist of a variety of asset classes, including shares of U.S. and foreign companies as well as bonds, cash and possibly alternative asset classes such as real estate investment trusts. That diverse mix means that you can't simply compare your portfolio's returns over various periods to the return of a single index that represents just one small segment of the financial markets. For example, many investors like to evaluate their portfolios' performance relative to the S&P 500 index. However, that index consists only of large companies located in the U.S. Unless your entire portfolio consists of just those types of firms, you would be "comparing apples to oranges" by using the S&P 500 as your benchmark. Instead, you'll want to try to compare your portfolio against the return of a composite index that is made up of different indices that more closely reflects your actual portfolio. Of course, this can be tricky if you have a number of different asset classes. Even so, an awareness of the issue is important.

It's also a good idea to compare your portfolio's returns to the expected rate of return that you determined you need to achieve your goals. This is the return that was calculated as part of your investment plan. Next, examine your portfolio's returns relative to the range of returns that you can reasonable expect your portfolio to produce over various time periods. For example, say your portfolio posted a return of -5 percent over the past 12 months. At first glance, that might not look so good. But say you learn through your review process that the all-time best 12-month return for a portfolio with your asset allocation was +25 percent and its worst 12-month return was -20 percent. That information tells you that your portfolio's -5 percent return is well within the normal range of returns that such a portfolio can be expected to deliver. Of course, no one wants to see their portfolio lose value—but in this case, you can be confident that your portfolio is behaving in line with expectations.

3. Adjust your plan, if necessary. As shown above, the best course of action in many cases is simply to do nothing and stick with your existing plan. That's why short-term performance data should be taken with a grain of salt. However, there are times when it can make sense to make changes to your plan and your portfolio. Say, for example, that you have a child who is just a few years away from starting college. In that case, it might make sense to shift some money from stocks to more stable investments such as bonds or cash that are less likely to lose their value in the short term. That way, you can be certain that the money to pay tuition will be there when you need it. Likewise, as you approach retirement, you may decide to adjust your asset allocation targets based on your needs and goals.

For clients who are retired or have cash needs, we like to set up a Cash Bucket account. This is a separate account to provide for the near-term cash needs of the client household. The Cash Bucket allows the client to separate the long-term portfolio from near-term cash needs both psychologically and physically, which provides additional peace of mind.

REBALANCING—A KEY ALLY IN YOUR LONG-TERM SUCCESS

Rebalancing is another reason why you might consider making adjustments to your portfolio.

To stay on track, you'll need to sell some of your investments and buy more of other investments every so often. That's because, as you've seen, various asset classes over time tend to move in different directions and at different magnitudes. For example, during times when stock prices soar, bond prices often decline. If that occurs for an extended period of time, your portfolio will become unbalanced—you will find yourself owning more stocks and fewer bonds than your plan calls for. When that happens, you might end up taking on more risk in your portfolio than you need to or than you comfortably tolerate. Remember from Chapter 7 that asset allocation is a huge driver of your long-term returns. That means you need to make sure your portfolio's asset allocation is where it needs to be.

That's where rebalancing comes in. Rebalancing helps you maintain a level of risk that is acceptable and appropriate for you given your situation. It also helps your build more wealth over time and better protect it. In addition, it provides you with a methodical system for following one of the most important investing concepts—buy low, sell high. That's because at its most basic, rebalancing means buying

more of the assets in your portfolio that have recently fallen in value and selling some of the assets in your portfolio that have recently risen.

This approach helps you consistently buy assets when they are priced low and sell some assets when they are priced high. The end result is that your portfolio will be in a much stronger position to generate the growth you need— without taking on more risk than you can handle. Indeed, one of the objectives of a portfolio that is efficiently rebalanced is to reduce the volatility of that portfolio and, hence, earn a greater risk-adjusted return. In addition, a disciplined rebalancing strategy will help you stay rational and avoid the classic and dangerous mistake of buying and selling based on the headlines in the media.

In general, it makes sense to rebalance a portfolio whenever any asset class allocation is off by more than 15 to 20 percent. For example, if your plan calls for a target stock allocation of 50 percent but your current allocation is actually 40 percent or less, you are now 20 percent below target for that asset class. Consequently, you would consider rebalancing back to your target by selling the appropriate amount of bonds or cash, or contributing new money from a cash account into stocks.

That said, general rules are exactly that—general. Because we limit our focus to a select few households, we are able to individually assess when each client's portfolio is ready to be (or should be) rebalanced. These tactical decisions may be a result of the accumulation of cash, the drift of asset class weightings, or the result of outside events such as a sudden collapse in the market. Each decision must be made by taking into account the client's household situation.

Intelligent rebalancing requires careful monitoring of performance and awareness of issues such as tax status, cash flow needs, financial goals and risk tolerance. Rebalancing can also generate transaction fees and costs associated with capital gains. In short, the benefits of rebalancing at a particular moment should outweigh the costs in order for you (or your advisor) to implement the rebalancing strategy.

While some rebalancing costs are unavoidable, there are ways to minimize the expense associated with rebalancing. For example:

1. Rebalance with new cash. The obvious way to rebalance is to sell some investments that have risen in value (and reallocate that money into investments that are below target). However, in a taxable account, that action can generate taxable capital gains. Therefore, a smart alternative approach is to use cash—such as new savings additions or excess cash in a savings or money market account—to buy new investments and to get your asset allocation back on track.

To enhance the efficiency of this process further, we rarely reinvest capital gains and dividends automatically. Reinvesting stock capital gains in a strong bull market merely adds to an already rich asset class. Instead, this cash flow is used to "value average" into the asset allocation, as described in item 4 below.

2. Rebalance at the household level using Tax Location to improve the tax and cost efficiency of the portfolio. By creating an asset allocation at the household level, we can assign asset class holdings to specific accounts based on their tax sensitivity. As a consequence, an IRA may be deliberately over-weighted in bonds while a taxable account is under-weighted in bonds but over-weighted in stock index funds, further reducing the tax footprint of the portfolio. This is known as tax location. It has the added benefit of reducing the total number of transactions required to rebalance, thereby reducing the frictional cost that results from trades.

3. Rebalance in tax-deferred accounts whenever possible. Selling investments in tax-deferred accounts such as 401(k)s will not incur a taxable gain. To the extent that rebalancing can occur in tax-advantaged accounts, you will sidestep taxes that would otherwise cut into your bottom line. This strategy is used in concert with tax location.

4. Engage in "Value Averaging." You are probably familiar with the concept of dollar-cost averaging. The benefit of this method is to lower the average cost structure of your portfolio. Unfortunately, dollar cost averaging has one glaring weakness: Fund capital gains and dividend distributions are naturally greatest at the end of a period of outperformance. Reinvesting at the top does not dovetail well with the concept of "buy low sell high."

Harvesting cash and periodically engaging in "bargain shopping" helps to avoid reinvesting at the top. That means seeking asset classes that are most advantageously priced and reinvesting the cash built-up solely in those attractive assets. This boosts the efficiency of reinvesting by focusing on relative and absolute value. This is called value averaging, and studies suggest that it boosts long-term returns.

5. Take advantage of Tax Loss Harvesting. Toward the end of each year, review your taxable accounts for any assets showing a possible capital loss. Those assets can be sold for a write-off, and immediately replaced if desired with relatively similar investments. Just be mindful of the "wash rule," which prevents you from recognizing a capital loss if the same, or substantially similar, security is purchased within 30 days before or after the sale.

Alternatively, if you have substantial tax loss carry-forwards, you might harvest a gain by selling an investment that has appreciated in value, and offset it against the carry-forward. These types of tax harvesting activities can add real value to portfolios in terms of after-tax (real net) returns.

CONCLUSION

Many investors who manage their investments on their own find it difficult to resist the urge to go on autopilot once they've built their portfolios. But as you have seen, it is extremely important for long-term investment success to regularly monitor your portfolio's performance relative to your goals. This is akin to monitoring your flight plan on a long flight.

You should also check in with yourself about any recent or upcoming developments that might impact your investment strategy. Armed with that information, you can make intelligent decisions about the right steps to take at all times—even if the right steps mean doing nothing at all with your portfolio and staying the course as your travel toward your destination.

CHAPTER 10

ADVANCED CASH MANAGEMENT™

THROUGHOUT THIS BOOK, WE'VE DISCUSSED the conundrum facing not just pilots, but most retail investors: lack of knowledge. If you had unlimited time, energy and resources, you might be able to manage your own portfolio after getting some practical investment management experience and earning a Certified Financial Planner™ (CFP®) credential. That would at least help you learn enough of the basics needed to separate the wheat from the chaff in the cacophony of conflicting advice you receive daily.

However, there's an easier, more practical way that's designed to address your key planning priorities. It's a consultative wealth management approach that enables the professional pilot (or other affluent professional) to engage a team of experts in the development of a plan to navigate his or her financial future. The next chapter of this book will fully describe a recommended wealth management approach.

Before we get there, however, there is one more important investment concept that needs to be explored: **Advanced Cash** Management.TM

WHAT IS ADVANCED CASH MANAGEMENT™?

Advanced Cash Management™ is a term coined by our firm that

refs to the placement and integration of client accounts and cash flows in such a manner as to simplify the client's income stream in retirement while creating behavioral buffers that protect the portfolio while simultaneously creating added piece of mind for the retiree.

WHY ADVANCED CASH MANAGEMENT™ IS IMPORTANT TO YOU

If you're planning on a dividend stream to get you through retirement, then you could have a problem with traditional stock dividends that are yielding just 2 percent these days. Moreover, bond yields are at historical lows. Advanced Cash Management™ provides sufficient cash income for your needs in an environment of low cash yields.

Piggybacking on the ideas of Kenneth French, one of the founding fathers of Modern Portfolio Theory who we've cited throughout this book, we can create "homemade" dividends and supplement them with pension income and social security income to maintain a minimum level of funding for your cash bucket. Your cash bucket is tapped for a constant income that is adjusted for inflation. In addition, your cash bucket provides a reserve for infrequent items such as property taxes or vacations.

It is our preference to implement Advanced Cash Management™ before you are retired. This gives us a reality check as to what you will "really" spend in retirement (subtracting direct employment-related expenses such as commuting). Ideally, when we flip the switch from your pre-retired stage of life to your "retired" stage of life, you won't even notice a difference from a cash-flow point of view. It's all handled under the cowling, behind the scenes. This is very important because people often face a "cash shock" when they first retire.

WHAT IS A REASONABLE DRAWDOWN AMOUNT FOR YOUR ASSETS?

In a widely cited study[1] about the longevity of retirement portfolios, researchers found that retirees who could limit their portfolio draws to 4 percent per year (plus inflation adjustments) were not likely to "outlive their money." In today's low-yield environment, however, some posit that a lower drawdown rate is more appropriate.

The aforementioned study, published in 1998 by Trinity University in San Antonio, Texas, is still relevant today. That's because the traditional "Four Percent Drawdown" rule doesn't apply when interest rates are very low and when people are routinely living 30 or more years into their retirement. While census data and mortality tables can give you fairly accurate predictors of one's *average* life expectancy, they just give you the average life expectancy— i.e. the age at which 50 percent of the people who share your genetic, hereditary, health and lifestyle habits will live beyond, and the age at which 50 percent will live below. Instead, as a starting point, you should set more conservative longevity targets for an age at which you have only, say, a 30 percent chance of living beyond.

> If you're interested in a more precise longevity estimate than you find in traditional longevity tables, visit LivingTo100.com where you can incorporate lifestyle factors into your longevity estimate.

Fortunately, additional research suggests that the early adoption and disciplined implementation of "guardrails" allows us to bring your safe withdrawal rate back up to the 4+ percent rate with inflation adjustments. What are guardrails? Simply put, they are your portfolio's alternate plan if your destination weather drops below specified minimums.

As our clients approach retirement, we spend significant time defining their cash income needs, the pre-tax draw required to meet those needs, and any guardrails adopted to protect the long-term viability of the disbursements. We call this a **disbursement policy** and it is incorporated into the **investment policy** of clients' needing income.

THE CASH BUCKET: A TWO-BUCKET APPROACH BASED ON BEHAVIORAL RESEARCH

Relying on research in behavioral finance, we have created two types of accounts, or buckets, as part of our Advanced Cash Management™ program.

1. **The first bucket** contains any accounts within your household investment portfolio.

2. **The second bucket** safeguards your emergency cash and cash income needs.

Your investment portfolio needs to be able to fund your cash bucket. Your cash bucket holds money that you may need to access in the next year or two— whether for emergencies, specific costs, or cash flow— and it must always be available to you.

HOW ADVANCED CASH MANAGEMENT™ WORKS

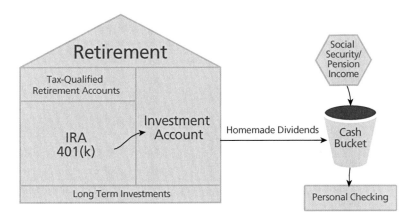

The house, in the graphic above, represents your investment portfolio at the household level. As we noted in Chapter 9, we recommend building your asset allocation at the household level to maximize tax efficiency while minimizing transaction costs.

As seen above, your household portfolio bucket includes your IRA, 401(k), tax qualified retirement plans (represented by the PRAP at UAL), and any joint, individual or trust/LLC/partnership accounts.

Homemade dividends are taken from the household bucket, deposited into the cash bucket and supplemented by social security, retirement income and any other outside income sources.

The cash bucket acts somewhat like a hydraulic reservoir, absorbing fluctuating inputs and generating a constant outflow of retirement, or even pre-retirement, cash income.

Why would we set this up before retirement? Because once you are retired, we have the infrastructure in place for a seamless transition from employment income to retirement income.

What is the behavioral impetus for adopting the cash bucket approach?

We split your funds into two buckets because the household investment bucket is going to move up and down over time. You can't put 100 percent of your money into bonds and draw down 3.5 percent to 4 percent annually when you have a 2.5 percent bond yield—**you need to grow your investments!**

However, if the market drops 30 percent— and it likely will, sooner or later— you won't have a heart attack. Why? Because you have separated your investment portfolio, physically and emotionally, from your cash needs account. It's comforting to know that you can rely on the cash bucket in the depths of a bear market, not touching your investments that need time to recover. When markets start to recover, you can then replenish the cash bucket with your investment portfolio.

GETTING STARTED WITH ADVANCED CASH MANAGEMENT™

Our Advanced Cash Management™ program has adopted strategies to harvest both cash interest and dividends as well as overvalued assets. We use what's known as **synthetic**, or **homemade, dividends** to allow the investment bucket to generate a relatively consistent income flow that feeds the cash bucket. Later in this chapter, we'll explore examples of homemade dividend techniques. For now, just understand that every month your retirement income is direct deposited from your cash bucket into your checking account. While you used to be paid by the airline for doing your job, you're now being "*paid*" by your portfolio to go out and enjoy your retirement.

The first step when setting up Advanced Cash Management™ is to set a budget. As noted previously, this step is best taken **before** you retire.

The best indicator of how much money you will need to live comfortably in each year of your retirement is based on how much money you are living on **now**—or think you'll be living on in the year **before** you retire.

There are exceptions of course—such as if you are trying to pay off your mortgage in the year before you retire. However, the most important concern is simulating your retirement cash flow as realistically as possible **before you retire**. If it turns out that you cannot live within a certain budget, then you will have a chance to revisit your plan before learning this lesson the hard way in retirement.

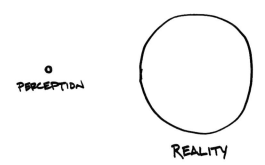

© 2013 Behavior Gap

DISBURSEMENT POLICY

As we discussed in Chapter 9, a good investment policy statement (IPS) should include the disbursement policy that's adopted once you retire. To that end, we've developed a method designed to give our clients a quantifiable level of confidence that they will never be in danger of outliving their money—no matter how volatile the markets, how much the cost of living rises or how frequently the tax rules change.

The disbursement policy is an important component of one's IPS but is frequently misunderstood by clients and can result in irrecoverable negative outcomes if mishandled.

Here's how. Unless your portfolio is making enough, over and above inflation, to survive the bad years, then you could easily find yourself going from a 4 percent or 5 percent withdrawal rate to a drawdown rate of 7 percent, 8 percent, 9 percent or even 10 percent! With withdrawal rates like that, after inflation and taxes, your portfolio is losing real (inflation adjusted) value rapidly. You've flown into a financial "death spiral" that's often not evident until, unfortunately, it's too late to recover.

At that point, you could be looking at a portfolio that's shrunk significantly when the initial market drop that triggered the "death spiral" was only 10 percent or 15 percent. Now, the only way that you can adapt is by taking a very substantial cut in your retirement income.

In this unpleasant scenario, if you had deferred social security and treated it as an insurance policy against things going wrong in your lump sum, then your situation might be less dire. In our experience, investors who make the first mistake (setting their withdrawal rate too high) often make the second mistake (taking social security as soon as they retire).

HOMEMADE (SYNTHETIC) DIVIDENDS

At the time this book was published (2014), we were in an era of high market returns, but also in a period of low bond returns, low interest rates and lowered expected returns. If you're retired or soon plan to be retired and are drawing down on your portfolio, does it make sense to constrain your spending to just the interest and dividends you receive?

The short answer is no. It shouldn't matter whether you spend capital gains or dividend and interest income.

Here's why: Suppose you are an investor in two companies of similar size, industry and customer focus. One of the companies chooses to use its earnings to pay dividends and the other company chooses to use its earnings to repurchase its shares. You could spend your dividends from the first company to fund your consumption. Alternatively, you could generate the same amount of money by selling some of your shares in the second company (i.e. the non-dividend paying one) and saving the rest.

Example: Suppose both companies have a share price of exactly $100 and they both generate $10 in earnings. The first company decides to pay out that $10 in earnings to shareholders. That generous dividend to shareholders will cause its stock price to fall by $10. Therefore, if you are an investor in that company, you've earned $10 in dividend and are now holding shares worth $90.

However, the other company decides to go out and repurchase some of its shares with its $10 in earnings. How many shares can it repurchase? Since the company's shares are worth $100, and the firm has $10 per share to repurchase, it can buy back one-tenth of their shares. If you, the investor, sell one-tenth of your shares, then for each of your shares, you have $10 in your pocket from selling back shares, and $90 left in the shares remaining. Either way, it's the same from an economic standpoint. Either you've earned $10 per share from the dividend paying company or you've created them yourself from the non-dividend paying company.

It's what famed economist Merton Miller used to call "home-made dividends."

There are more advanced strategies you can use, such as "covered calls," but they have the disadvantage of added complexity and carry a cost. It is debatable whether or not covered calls add anything more than simply a psychological advantage. Therefore, they are not addressed here.

Go to http://www.efficientwealthmanagement.com/who-we-are/media/videos/ for an informative video with renowned financial economist Kenneth French about homemade dividends (courtesy of Dimensional Fund Advisors).

WHY A HIGH STOCK DIVIDEND/BOND YIELD STRATEGY CAN DISTORT A PORTFOLIO

So, why do some investors prefer high dividend paying companies? For some investors, it's a way to constrain themselves. They might think they have spending control problems or they may just think it's a good rule of thumb not to "invade" their principal. The problem with this logic is that it can cause you to distort your portfolio. For example, if you are spending your dividends and interest (or your advisor is allowing you to), and you know want to spend more money, then you might want to "tilt" toward companies that pay a lot of dividends. Or you might tilt toward bonds that pay a lot of interest. The result might be a portfolio that's less well diversified or that doesn't have all the great characteristics that it might otherwise have if you just ignored this problem and said: "I'll make synthetic or homemade dividends for myself."

What about the fixed income investor who might want bonds that offer higher yields?

It's really clear when you look at the fixed income market how an investor might distort their portfolio by chasing the higher interest just because they might want to consume (i.e. spend more money) from a high yielding portfolio. Conventional wisdom is that you can get those higher interest payments by going out and buying riskier bonds— i.e. bonds that are more likely to default. If the economy remains strong and everything works out real well, then you'll get those higher yields and you will be able to consume and spend more.

Unfortunately, if the economy slips into a recession while you're holding those riskier bonds, the companies backing those bonds might default on them and you'll really regret this decision. In an effort to get more liquid cash to consume, you'll actually end up losing money.

It is our philosophy that the return for excess risk is greater in equities than it is in bonds. There are some exceptions, such as when specific bond asset classes are priced substantially below their long-run averages. However, in general, risk belongs in equities. Bonds are for portfolio stability and for surviving turbulent periods.

REBALANCING TO CASH AS A MECHANISM FOR CREATING HOMEMADE DIVIDENDS

We discussed rebalancing extensively in the last chapter. Remember that over time, as the market moves and as various investments in your portfolio rise or fall, the value of those investments, and, thus the allocation of the assets within your portfolio, is likely to change. **For example**, say your investment policy states you should allocate no more than 30 percent of your portfolio to stocks. However, after a rise in the stock market and a fall in bond values, the value of your stock portfolio might increase to 36 percent of your assets. You must adjust or rebalance your portfolio by selling stocks and buying bonds and moving a portion of your assets to cash.

Rebalancing allows you to prevent your portfolio from becoming too risky or too conservative. However, rebalancing may hurt overall returns because the process tends to result in selling better performing assets and in buying underperforming assets. When you rebalance, you throttle-back your risk exposure. Naturally that modestly impacts long-term returns.

Therefore, rebalancing should not be done too frequently, and it should only be done when the variance from the asset allocation targets is high. This has the added benefit of allowing us to harvest the "momentum" effect.

In the low interest rate environments, such as when this book was originally published in 2014, an obsession with income-oriented investments may lead to unnecessary portfolio distortion and hence unexpected risk within the portfolio.

Advanced Cash Management™ solves the issue of retirement cash need without unnecessarily biasing your portfolio toward companies with higher dividend yields or toward bonds with higher yields to maturity. This negates putting the cart before the horse; letting the income tail wag the portfolio dog.

Once your overall asset allocation decision has been made on the basis of total portfolio risk and return, your income produced becomes a by-product. In many cases, if you're a taxable investor, you are better off reducing your income and periodically selling securities to meet the balance of your cash flow needs. However, a concept called "mental accounting"—in which people tend to separate their money into different mental buckets—seems to be a powerful force preventing this approach.

An example of mental accounting, based on the intended use of funds, is when an investor puts money for a child's education into a low interest earning savings account yet carries a balance on a high interest credit card. Here, the importance of the intended use of the money (i.e., education) means it is not used to pay off expensive debt, even when doing so results in a net economic benefit.

Satisfying the need for mental accounting comes at the expense of higher taxes or the desire for a portfolio that may not be appropriate for investors' risk tolerance. Behavioral finance guru, Meir Statman, argues that investors prefer dividends because the regular payment provides a simple self-control rule: Live off the dividend, but don't touch the principal[2]. The dividend becomes like an allowance, whereas, if firms repurchase shares, the investor must periodically sell shares to raise cash. The economic impact before taxes is the same, but there wouldn't be a designated amount to view as an allowance, and the share sales could be seen as a dip into principal.

Deena Katz, CFP®, professor at Texas Tech University and a principal in the Miami firm of Evensky & Katz has long advocated adopting a *five-year mantra*: Five years, five years, five years. What she means is that you do not want to invest in long-term assets any funds that you expect to need for your big purchases in the next five years. Those funds should be placed in cash, near-cash or short-term bonds. There is simply too much risk that in a few years when you need the money the market will be down.

For retirement cash flow, Katz is also a big proponent of *setting aside up to two years' worth of your required cash flow* in a fashion similar to the cash bucket that we recommended here. This way, you can draw down your regular living expenses on a monthly basis from that liquid account. When the market is in turmoil (as today), you may not be happy; however, you will not have to sell as your grocery money is sitting in cash and you will not have lost a penny. By placing you, the investor, not the market, in control of when to sell investments, this strategy will minimize much of the risk associated with market volatility.

If market volatility has taught us anything over the past decade, it is that rules of thumb, such as the Four Percent Drawdown Rule are only useful as starting points for developing your financial plan. Just as weather and flight conditions constantly change, financial security in retirement is likely to be a shifting target that is influenced by many largely unpredictable factors.

Just as economic pressures continue to change, the thinking about retirement withdrawal rates continues to evolve. Rules of thumb may be useful and educational, but they are no substitute for a detailed, personalized retirement plan that is monitored frequently and adjusted as conditions demand.

In the next chapter, we'll look closer at the comprehensive wealth management process and how pilots can engage a well-rounded team of experts to help them navigate their financial futures.

1 Cooley, Philip L.; Hubbard, Carl M. and Walz, Daniel T. "Retirement Savings: Choosing a Withdrawal Rate That Is Sustainable" *AAII Journal,* February 1998 http://www.aaii.com/journal/article/retirement-savings-choosing-a-withdrawal-rate-that-is-sustainable

2 Statman, Meir "Behavioral Finance versus Standard Finance" AAII Finance.com http://www.aiinfinance.com/Statman.pdf

CHAPTER 11

THE WEALTH MANAGEMENT CONSULTATIVE PROCESS

THE BULK OF THIS BOOK HAS BEEN FOCUSED on what we have found to be our clients' overwhelming top financial concern: how best to position investment capital to grow wealth, to protect it during difficult market environments and to make it last for a lifetime.

As crucial as an intelligent investing strategy is to your future financial success, it is not the only component in a truly effective flight plan for wealth.

The fact is, as an investor with significant means, you need an approach to managing your wealth that is not scattershot but truly comprehensive in nature—an entire framework for making intelligent decisions, not just about your investments but also the advanced challenges that today's affluent investors face. To address all of the key issues of importance in your life, you also need the right team of experts working with you side-by-side, to coordinate advice into a single comprehensive strategy.

I call this approach wealth management, and this chapter will provide you with an overview of how wealth management—true wealth management—will put you in the best possible position to achieve all that is most important to you.

WHAT IS A TRUE WEALTH MANAGER?

Let's be honest: Many in the financial services industry like to call themselves wealth managers these days. However, most simply offer basic investment management services—not the type of comprehensive and coordinated approach that will help you and your extended family achieve your life goals.

Consider the facts: A study of more than 2,000 financial advisors by advisor research firm CEG Worldwide found that just 6.6 percent are actually wealth managers. The remaining 93.4 percent are investment generalists who take a much more limited and simplistic approach with clients[1].

Figure 11.1 The Business Models of Financial Advisors

Wealth managers 6.6%

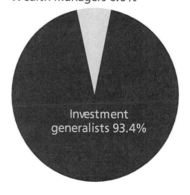

Source: CEG Worldwide.

So how will you know whether you are dealing with a true wealth manager? Look for the following characteristics:

1. Your advisor should offer a consultative, comprehensive wealth management process. wealth management means having your financial challenges solved and your financial situation enhanced by bringing together ideas and solutions to encompass all types of financial needs throughout all phases of your financial life. To accomplish this, a true Wealth manager will deliver a process consisting of three primary components:

- *Investment Consulting.* As noted above, growing and protecting wealth is the number one concern that most affluent investors have today. Therefore, investment consulting is the core offering for many wealth managers and the foundation upon which they build a comprehensive wealth management plan.

- *Advanced Planning.* Advanced planning addresses the range of financial needs beyond investment consulting that are important to affluent investors. Advanced planning consists of four areas: **wealth enhancement** (mitigating taxes and keeping more wealth in your pocket), **wealth transfer** (taking care of your heirs based on your wishes and on the best wealth transfer strategies), **wealth protection** (making sure your hard-earned wealth is not unjustly taken from you) and **charitable gifting** (having a meaningful effect on the world at large and supporting causes about which you are passionate). Few financial professionals provide these services in meaningful ways.

- *Relationship Management.* Relationship management works in concert with advanced planning and involves three key tasks: first, **fully understanding clients' critical needs** and meeting those needs over time through a consultative process; second, **assembling and managing a network of financial experts** who are ideally suited to implement advanced planning strategies; and third, **working effectively with affluent clients' other professional advisors**, such as attorneys and accountants.

2. Your advisor should act as your "personal CFO." A personal Chief Financial Officer is someone who has the expertise and experience to identify the full range of the financial challenges that you and your family face, and who can develop the optimal solutions that work in concert with each other. An advisor who adopts the role of a personal CFO will identify your true financial needs and goals; craft a long-range wealth management plan that will meet those needs and goals; and build an ongoing relationship that ensures your needs continue to be met as they change over time. It's also the job of a personal CFO to oversee and manage the efforts of those professionals who will implement advanced planning strategies related to wealth enhancement, wealth transfer, wealth protection and charitable gifting.

3. Your advisor should be credentialed. The gold standard for financial planning advice is the Certified Financial Planner™ (CFP®) credential. The CFP® is a graduate-level credentialing program that requires a minimum amount of college experience, passing a difficult battery of exams that covers six major areas of investment and financial planning, and at least three years of supervised full-time experience. In addition, some formal education in finance, economics, or investment analysis suggests a professional orientation and investment in the clients' future.

It's important to note that being *credentialed* is **not** the same as being *licensed*. Remarkably, the Series 63 or Series 65 certifications held by most "investment advisors" are focused primarily on compliance regulations and don't require much investment understanding. A reasonably intelligent individual, with no financial background and the appropriate preparatory material, could study and pass these tests in a matter of weeks.

4. Your advisor should be held to a fiduciary standard of care. A core tenet of the CFP® Board's Code of Ethics is that the client's best interests should come first—ahead of the interests of the advisor. This is called the fiduciary standard of care. This somewhat esoteric definition can be clarified by considering the effects of an agency relationship with a broker whose legal standard of care is "do no harm," thereby allowing commissions to drive the advice given.

This has become an area of such concern that the SEC is considering applying a fiduciary standard to all advisors. Meanwhile, the commission-oriented advice industry is lobbying furiously to water-down the same fiduciary standard to limit the damage of such a change. Now, it is possible to be a fiduciary and also receive commissions. However, even for the most honest practitioner, it's difficult for one's recommendations not to dovetail with one's income. Consequently, many fiduciary advisors have adopted a fee-only model.

WHY WEALTH MANAGEMENT?

The true Wealth Management approach that we deliver has important advantages over methods used by other advisors. For example:

1. Wealth Management uses a consultative process to establish close relationships with clients in order to gain a detailed understanding of their goals and their most important financial wants and needs.

2. Wealth Management offers customized choices and solutions designed to fit each individual's needs. This range of interrelated financial services and products might include, for example, investment management, insurance, estate planning and retirement planning.

3. Wealth Management delivers these customized solutions in close consultation with clients and their other professional advisors. A wealth manager works closely with you and your other professional advisors on an ongoing basis to identify your specific needs, design custom solutions to meet those needs and "quarterback" the entire process to ensure optimal results at every step.

Here's how wealth management benefits pilots, specifically. As a result of previously discussed industry uncertainty and behavioral challenges, the vast majority of pilots interviewed said they felt under-prepared for retirement. They shared common concerns that are, in many cases, not addressed by a traditional investment management program. However, these concerns can be addressed by wealth management.

Transitioning to retirement is, in many ways, much like preparing for a long flight. As you start your journey, you'll want to know your "release fuel" —what's your probable burn to reach your desired retirement? Are you building in enough reserve should you need to divert to an alternate or contingency destination (in the event of medical or other issues)? What are your "divert options?" In the event you see weather ahead, who will be there to provide you with input on conditions at your alternate destination?

Much like a dispatch release, your flight plan for retirement should tell you how much fuel you will burn, keep you abreast of changing conditions, and present adequate alternate options for unforeseen circumstances.

To create your plan, you need to lay out your ultimate destination, identify the areas of uncertainty and risk that may affect your ability to achieve them, and create a strategy for dealing with each.

Such a wide range of financial needs requires a wide range of financial expertise. Because no one person can be an expert in all of these subjects, the best Wealth managers serve as your personal Chief Financial Officer (CFO), bringing together a team of experts—professionals with deep experience and knowledge in specific fields.

Pilots are known to be independent, capable, hands-on people. Many try to go it alone when it comes to planning for retirement. However, Wealth Management is a very complex process, not unlike flying a jet. You wouldn't pretend not to need dispatch, maintenance or a flight crew. You wouldn't disregard your flight plan or ignore the pre-flight checklist.

Nor should you be any less methodical with something as important as your own retirement. You need someone who can give you your best alternative in the event of financial "bad weather." You're still the Captain; you're just relying on others to perform the specialized roles they excel in so you may focus on what you do best.

DOES YOUR WEALTH MANAGEMENT PLAN HAVE ENOUGH LIFT?

- **L**egal Strategy – Estate Planning and Risk Management

- **I**nsurance Protection – Personal and Life

- **F**inance – Investment Management and Retirement Planning

- **T**ax Mitigation – Maximize Deductions, Spend Less Time

THE WEALTH MANAGEMENT PROCESS

The consultative wealth management process outlined above typically is implemented over a series of meetings:

1. **A Discovery Meeting** in which you discuss your current financial situation, your goals and the obstacles you face in achieving them. Without this knowledge, the best investment and advanced planning solutions in the world won't do much good. The goal of the discovery meeting is to identify your unique situation on a deep level so that the optimal plan can be designed.

2. **An Investment Plan Meeting** in which the wealth manager presents a complete diagnostic of your current financial situation and an investment plan for achieving your investment-related goals. This plan serves as the roadmap that will enable you to preserve and grow your wealth.

3. **A Mutual Commitment Meeting** in which you and the wealth manager agree to work together. At this point, the wealth manager effectively becomes your personal Chief Financial Officer, and the investment plan is put into action.

4. **An Initial Follow-Up Meeting** in which the wealth manager helps you to organize your new account paperwork and answers the inevitable questions that occur after the wealth management process is implemented.

5. **Recurring Regular Progress Meetings,** the first of which involves the presentation of the advanced plan—the comprehensive flight plan developed in coordination with the network of insurance, legal, and tax experts. During subsequent meetings, your wealth manager will discuss your progress toward your goals and recommend any necessary "heading" changes.

Figure 11.2: The Consultative Wealth Management Process

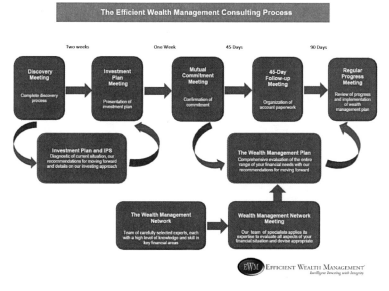

CONCLUSION

As an affluent pilot, you face financial challenges and possess financial goals that demand true wealth management. Simplistic solutions that focus only on one area of your financial life are neither adequate nor appropriate for someone in your position.

True wealth management is designed not only to address all of the key areas of importance to you, but also to manage those areas in a coordinated and integrated manner—using the full range of experts and resources that are necessary to get you to your goals on time and with as much peace of mind as possible.

1 John J. Bowen, Paul Brunswick, & Jonathan Powell. "Breaking Through: Building a World-Class Wealth Management Business. " *CEG Worldwide, LLC*

FLIGHT PLAN FOR WEALTH
CONCLUSION

AT THE BEGINNING OF THIS BOOK, I stated that you need a framework for making intelligent financial decisions—in all areas of your financial life, and at every stage.

You now have that framework and have learned the key strategies that a select group of today's most successful investors use to grow and protect their wealth. You also know the right process for coordinating the most important non-investment components of your financial life—from mitigating taxes and safeguarding their assets to making intelligent and effective estate and charitable plans.

As you have seen, these strategies—collectively known as **consultative wealth management**—will empower you to address your biggest financial challenges, needs and objectives as an airline industry professional. For example, remember that our survey revealed that fully 93 percent of pilots are not satisfied with their retirement preparation. You owe it to yourself and your family to be in the select seven percent who *are* prepared.

Our consultative wealth management approach, implemented with a team of credentialed experts, enables you to take back command of your financial future and achieve your goals with clarity and confidence. By integrating familiar crew resource management skills into the financial planning process, a true wealth manager can be your financial First Officer—your personal CFO—and give you the edge you need.

If you are currently working with a financial advisor, but are unsure whether all aspects of your retirement plan have been adequately addressed, then seek out a second opinion from a consultative wealth manager. A true wealth manager will conduct a Discovery Meeting, as previously described, and present you with a roadmap to success in retirement and in all your key life endeavors.

Whether you're looking for help or just a second opinion, one resource that enables you to find advisors and critically examine their credentials is the Financial Planning Association (FPA) at www.fpanet.org. The FPA is the largest membership organization for personal financial planning experts in the U.S. and includes professionals from all backgrounds and business models. The FPA can help connect you to a competent and ethical planner who upholds the FPA Standard of Care.

THE FINANCIAL PLANNING ASSOCIATION STANDARD OF CARE

All financial planning services will be delivered in accordance with the following standard of care:

- Put the client's best interests first;

- Act with due care and in utmost good faith

- Do not mislead clients

- Provide full and fair disclosure of all material facts and

- Disclose and fairly manage all material conflicts of interest.

Ultimately, you have the power to put yourself and your wealth on the right flight plan. The decision is yours. Do you wish to continue to invest and plan "as usual", or do you prefer to implement the key strategies that have generated hugely successful results?

Take some time to consider what you have just read, and ask yourself if you are currently making the optimal decisions about your wealth—or if perhaps there is a better way that can maximize your ability to achieve all that is truly most important to you and your family.

If you choose to bring wealth management into your financial life, the best thing you can do is act today. The sooner your flight plan is filed and your crew is onboard, the greater your opportunity to improve the quality of your journey.

Have a safe flight!

CONTENTS

1. UAL PILOT RETIREMENT INFORMATION

The UAL MEC R&I Committee developed this retirement checklist in order to answer any questions you might have regarding the retirement process and your benefits. As you get closer to retirement, you will want to make sure to contact the required agencies at the appropriate time prior to retirement to prevent disruption of your benefits.

Please note that rates and quotes change frequently. Always consider UAL information to be most current. To some extent, I have deliberately avoided certain specifics, as the facts would be stale by printing.

I. RETIREMENT NOTIFICATION PROCESS

As far as the Company is concerned, it is assumed that you will fly until mandatory retirement age of 65. If you would like to retire early, you must notify the Company in writing of the date you plan to retire. This letter should include retirement date, file number and your signature, and should be turned in to your Chief Pilot's office.

For pilots who retire early, your PSNL page in Unimatic will be updated to reflect your new status and you will be removed from the bidding roster for the month following your retirement. There is no specific deadline for notifying the Company of your intent to retire early. Nevertheless, we suggest that you do so after you have made a definite decision to retire early and, ideally, at least one full bid period prior to the date you intend your retirement to be effective. At a minimum, you should give the Company at least 10 calendar days' notice in order to ensure that you will be paid for vacation accrued during the current vacation year (Section 11-B).

II. FINAL PAY

If you are retiring at age 65, you will be paid through your last trip flown. However, you cannot fly past midnight local domicile time the night before your birthday. If you have a carry over into the next month, you will be paid up to midnight on the last day of the pilot month and you will not be paid the carryover time. The pay between your 65th birthday and the end of the month will be at 2.8 hours per day for every day, including days off. The Company recently unilaterally changed this past practice so that the 2.8 hours per day after your 65th birthday is not paid. ALPA is currently grieving this issue.

For early retirements, you can retire on any day in the month. However, after your last trip you will be on no-pay status until the end of that month. If you retire early but work until the end of a given month, you will be paid through the last trip. If the last trip has carryover to the next month, it will be dropped with no pay. You are considered to be retired on the first day of the month following your last month of flying. Since we are paid in arrears, you will receive a paycheck on the 1st and 16th of the month following your retirement.

III. VACATION PAY

Your vacation will be paid out in the following manner:

- The first 21 days will be an employer contribution to the PRAP.
- Any vacation days in excess of 21 will be converted to cash and you will receive a paper check mailed to your home of record.

Vacation value is determined as 3.25 multiplied by the number of days multiplied by your hourly rate. Make sure your home of record address is current and you should receive the check approximately three weeks after your retirement date.

IV. MISCELLANEOUS PAY

All expenses (e.g. dry cleaning, parking, meals) should be turned in at least two weeks prior to your effective retirement date. This will allow payroll time to process your expenses in a timely manner.

V. LAST FLIGHT

You may contact the Chief Pilot's Office Staff Representative for help with your final trip and positive space for your spouse or domestic partner. Other individuals will need to buy a ticket on your retirement flight. Return to your Chief Pilot's Office any parking tags, crew badge, airport badge, known crew member badge, Ipad and other related materials.

VI. LTD OPT-OUT

Make sure you opt-out of the LTD Plan at least 90 days prior to your retirement date. Since there is a 90 day waiting period to commence LTD benefits, and since benefits automatically end at retirement, paying premiums within 90 days of retirement will be paying a premium for nothing. The only caveat about this is, if you're retiring early, and you aren't absolutely certain you won't change your mind, you may not want to opt out; if you opt out and then decide to revoke your notice of early retirement, you may need to show evidence of insurability to get back into the LTD Plan. To opt-out of the LTD plan contact the Benefits Service Center at 1-800-651-1007.

VII. RETIREMENT INCOME

A. New PRAP

When you retire, you will have multiple options regarding your PRAP account. First and foremost, you can leave your assets in the PRAP, continue to direct their investment as you always have and begin distributions for living expenses as necessary. Similar to an IRA, required minimum distributions (RMD) are required beginning no later than April 1st of the year after the year you turn 70 ½. The Auto PRAP Retirement Fund is a simple, cost effective and well diversified option designed to be an appropriate choice for pilots post-retirement.

Another option is to purchase an annuity using assets from your PRAP account(s). You would be buying a future monthly income in exchange for some, or all, of your PRAP account. This is the legally-required default distribution option within the PRAP, however it is rarely used.

If desired, you can roll over your PRAP account to another financial institution when you retire. If you decide to roll over your money to a different institution, you might want to wait until you receive your final paycheck so that all of your final deposits are made into your PRAP account before you make the transfer. You can contact Schwab directly at 1-866-OUR-PRAP or use the website to obtain the appropriate forms.

Each option has different associated costs and fees and you should carefully consider the advantages and disadvantages prior to making any decisions. As always, we strongly recommend that you consult your financial and tax advisors in making your decisions. If you choose to stay in the PRAP, be sure to keep your designation of beneficiary up to date to take into account any change in your family or other circumstances after your retirement.

B. PBGC

You should contact the PBGC three months prior to the date you want to commence PBGC benefits. However, you can call them anytime if you simply want to determine your estimated anticipated benefits for future retirement planning. The R&I Committee and the PBGC strongly recommend that pilots get PBGC benefit estimates at different ages so that pilots can make an informed decision of when to take their PBGC benefit.

The earliest you can collect from PBGC while continuing to work for UAL is age 60 but by delaying the initiation of your PBGC benefits your benefit amount will most likely increase. While this is true for almost all currently active UAL pilots, it is not true in 100 percent of cases. So, at the point you are deciding whether to start your PBGC benefit right away or to wait until later, you should ask the PBGC not only what your benefit will be if you begin it immediately, but also what it will be if you start it at one or more future dates.

If you decide to retire before age 60 (PBGC retirement age), you will need to give the PBGC 3 pieces of information:

1. Proof of termination of employment from United Airlines

2. Proof of age such as a copy of birth certificate or passport (note that you cannot use your driver's license)

3. Copy of marriage certificate, if applicable

There is no "correct" answer whether to receive PBGC benefits at age 60, wait until age 65 or 70, or take it at some other age. It is dependent on each individual pilot's circumstances. Some factors to consider are your health, your projected longevity and personal financial situation. Many pilots will receive the PC-4 guarantee (your situation might be different). The straight life annuity monthly maximum guarantee for plans that terminated in 2004 (our A-plan terminated in 2004) is:

- Age 60: $2,404.26
- Age 65: $3,698.86

There are many different options for payments from the PBGC and benefit determination letters will spell out the different choices and associated benefit levels (for example, Straight-life annuity, Joint and 50 percent Survivor Annuity, Joint and 75 percent Survivor Annuity, Joint and 100 percent Survivor Annuity, etc.). Please take the time to learn about the different options prior to making a decision about the best option for you and your family.

PBGC Contact Information

1-800-400-7242
Case #: 19962700 (Legacy United)
www.pbgc.gov

VIII. RETIREE HEALTH INSURANCE

A. DENTAL

Dental coverage ends on the last day of the month in which you end your employment. You might consider getting all necessary dental work done prior to your retirement. COBRA will be offered for 18 months after your retirement and you can sign up for one month, two months, etc. up to 18 months.

B. VISION

Vision coverage ends on the last day of the month in which you end your employment. You can continue vision coverage by using COBRA for up to 18 months or any part thereof. The cost of the vision will go up 2 percent with COBRA.

C. MEDICAL INSURANCE

Pilots who have attained at least age 50 with 10 or more years of service are eligible to continue medical insurance with UAL during retirement. Pilots will continue to receive active medical plan benefits through the end of their retirement month. For example, if a pilot turns 65 on March 5th, he will have active medical till March 31st. On the first of the next month, the pilot will be covered by the Before or After Medicare plan, depending on his age.

A retiree will receive a packet of health insurance information from the United Benefit Service Center. A retiree can expect to receive this package 30 days after his retirement date. A pilot can also call the Benefits Service Center or go on YBR within 90 days of his retirement date and model different retiree medical plans to better understand his choices before retirement.

When a retiree enrolls in the medical plan as a retiree, United will pay the first two months of his health insurance premiums and he will be covered retroactively to his retirement date. It is beneficial to enroll as soon as possible after retiring so that there will not be a disruption in coverage. Even though medical plan coverage will be retroactive to the pilot's retirement date, any medical costs incurred between the pilot's retirement date and the date coverage is reestablished will require filing for reimbursement for medical costs which could be substantially more paperwork intensive than having coverage established at retirement.

A retiree can call the Benefits Service Center at 1-800-651-1007 or go on YBR to enroll in a retiree medical plan even if the health insurance packet has not arrived. **If a retiree does not enroll in medical coverage, medical coverage will cease on his retirement date and there will not be two free months of coverage.** To keep the option of returning to the UAL medical plan, a retiree can "suspend" coverage (24-F-2-d) when first eligible for coverage or during Annual Enrollment. If the retiree suspends coverage he can return to the UAL medical plan at a later date. If a retiree desires to "suspend" coverage, contact the Benefits Service Center at 1 800-651-1007 or select "No Coverage" as a medical plan option on the YBR. If a retiree waives coverage he can never return to the UAL medical plan.

If retired and not using the UAL medical plan, always suspend coverage so you have the option to come back into the plan. To return to the UAL medical plan, a retiree who "suspended" coverage will need to provide the Benefits Service Center a certificate of creditable coverage establishing proof of continuous coverage under a group health plan, Medigap–Plan J, Tri-Care or a Medicare HMO during the period for which retiree medical coverage was suspended.

Retirees who elect to continue medical coverage after retirement participate in the annual open enrollments just as they did before retirement. Depending on their age, they will be able to select from among the before-Medicare or after-Medicare Benefits.

*Spouse/Dependents are only covered under the UAL medical plan if the pilot stays in the UAL medical plan.

If you have a life event (marriage, dependents, etc.) you can add these new additions to your family to your insurance if you apply within 45 days of the life event. If a retiree has suspended coverage, a life event will enable the retiree to reenter the medical plan within this 45 day period. In the absence of a life event, a retiree who has suspended coverage needs to wait until open enrollment to re-enter the plan. You will pay for your medical insurance every month. You can choose to receive a payment coupon or set up an auto-withdrawal from a bank account. To learn more about these options contact the Benefits Service Center at 1-800-651-1007 or go to the YBR at Flying Together > Employee Services > Benefits > Your Benefit Resources. However you make payments, do not be late making your payments. Being more than 30 days late on your payments can be grounds for loss of medical benefits.

Before-Medicare Medical Benefits:

If a retiree is under age 65 he will be in a before-Medicare Plan. All plans that are available to active pilots are available for retirees in the before-Medicare Plans. The premiums for retirees are greater than active pilots. Retirees pay the following percentages of the plan costs based on their years of service at retirement:

Years of Service	Percentage of Cost
Fewer than 20	80%
20 to 25	60%
25 and over	40%

Active pilots in the PPO pay 20 percent of the cost. Therefore retired pilots with over 25 years of service would see their PPO contributions double, pilots with 20-25 years would see their PPO contributions triple and those with fewer than 20 years would see their PPO contributions quadruple. Even the maximum pre-Medicare rates are believed to compare favorably to individually available pre- Medicare commercial insurance health coverage.

After-Medicare Medical Benefits:

If a retiree is age 65 or older, the pilot will be in an after-Medicare Plan. Medicare will be the primary payer and the UAL after-Medicare plans will be the secondary payer. UAL is required to offer at least one supplemental plan to Medicare. They currently offer three. (Some pilots are also eligible for HMO(s) depending on where they live.) UAL contributes $90 per month per covered individual in an After-Medicare plan. The pilot pays the remaining amount. Pilots can currently choose between the following plans (their 2013 premiums are listed):

Medical Plans

You can learn more about these plans and their plan design by logging into Skynet (not Flying Together), Employee Services, Benefits, Plan Summaries – Retirees. *Coverage Methodology.*

Retiree Pilot and Spouse Both Under age 65

Both would be covered under the before-Medicare Plan.

Retiree Pilot over age 65 and Spouse under age 65

Pilot covered under the after-Medicare Plan (you only), Spouse under before-Medicare plan (you only). If they have children, spouse and children covered under before-Medicare plan (you and child(ren)).

Retiree Pilot under age 65 and Spouse over age 65

Pilot covered under before-Medicare Plan (you only or you and child(ren), if applicable). Spouse covered under after-Medicare Plan (you only)

Retiree Pilot and Spouse over age 65

Both covered under after-Medicare Plan (you and spouse)

Active Pilot with Spouse over age 65

Both covered under active medical plan.

IX. RETIREE HEALTH ACCOUNT (RHA)

The RHA is a tax efficient way to pay for retiree medical expenses. All pilots have an RHA with at least some funds available to them. Save your unreimbursed medical expenses (including your postretirement medical contributions for before- and after-Medicare benefits) after the date you retire. No later than January 1, 2014, retired pilots will be able to be reimbursed from the RHA for qualified medical expenses they have incurred after retirement. Medical and dental contributions, out of pocket medical and dental costs and long-term care premiums are just some examples of the medical costs that can be reimbursed.

X. LIFE INSURANCE

Company paid life insurance will cease when a pilot retires. To convert your Company paid life insurance into an individual policy contact Metlife at 1-877-275-6387.

XI. OTHER

A. CREDIT UNION

If you're using the Alliant Credit Union (or any bank, for that matter) to pay your bills because you had your UAL paycheck deposited there, make sure that your future payments (Social Security, PBGC, retirement account disbursements, etc.) are deposited in such a way to cover your future bills now that you won't have a United Airlines paycheck going into that account anymore.

B. TRAVEL BENEFITS

Retirees no longer receive higher boarding priorities due to their years of service unless using a vacation pass. A complete summary of retiree pass travel privileges can be found by clicking the "Travel" tab on Flying Together, then locating the "Additional Information" section in the middle of the page. Then, click on "Retiree Pass Travel Privileges" to open a PDF outlining all of your retirement travel benefits in detail.

Retirees with 25 or more years of active service, and their eligible pass riders, receive fee-waived pass travel in all cabins system wide. On January 1st, eligible retirees will be issued 8, one-way family vacation ePasses for higher boarding (SA0V) priority, space available travel. If not using a vacation ePass, boarding priority will be SA2R or lower. This is one priority class lower than active employees. Retirees can register up to two enrolled friends in addition to a spouse/domestic partner. Retirees are still eligible to purchase "regular" tickets on United at a 20 percent discount Retirees will use their badge through its expiration date for travel. After the badge expires, retiree eligibility letters will be required. Retirees will pre-pay all service charges and taxes for themselves and eligible pass riders with a credit card on employeeRES at the time booking is made.

If your travel plans change, cancel your booking through employeeRES prior to the travel date for an automatic refund. If your booking is not cancelled prior to the travel date, allow 5-7 days for a refund. If you pay for a premium seat and sit in economy, refund requests are made online at www.united.com > reservations > refund.

Retirees and their spouse or domestic partner are eligible for free emergency, positive-space roundtrip travel when either of you becomes ill while traveling. Contact the Employee Travel Center Monday through Friday from 8:00 – 5:00 P.M. at 1-713-324-5555, option number 5 or at ETC@united.com. For questions regarding policies and program information, you can contact the United Employee Travel Center at ETC@united.com.

C. RETIREMENT PICTURE

United will not pay for your retirement aircraft photograph. If you would like to purchase a photo for your fellow pilots to sign, you will need to order it yourself. You should check with your flight office if they recommend someone or have negotiated a special rate with certain photographers.

D. RETIRED UNITED PILOT ASSOCIATION (RUPA)

RUPA is a central point for retirees to continue the camaraderie of flying the line. RUPA has local groups of retirees who meet monthly throughout the U.S. They publish a monthly magazine and keep their website up-to-date on various issues - especially pass travel issues and health benefits. To learn more about RUPA visit their website at www.RUPA.org.

2. GOVERNMENT BENEFITS

A. SOCIAL SECURITY

Contact the Social Security department at www.socialsecurity.gov to commence your Social Security benefit. As of 2013, you must be at least 61and 9 months old to apply. You should apply no more than four months prior to your requested start. If you are over 62, benefits could start the month you apply (retroactively, where appropriate). If you want to estimate what your future Social Security retirement benefits will be, you can go to www.socialsecurity.gov/estimator. The Social Security website is robust and you can model different payments and try to understand when is the most beneficial time to commence benefits for you and your spouse (if applicable).

There are literally hundreds of different benefit options available and diligence is required prior to making decisions that could have a substantial impact on your benefit. Your health and projected longevity are important factors in your decision process. There has been considerable research on Social Security maximizing strategies. Two of the most popular strategies are the "claim and suspend" and the "restricted application" (also referred to as the "free spousal benefit" or the "claim now claim later strategy").

There are a number of websites and documents on the Internet that can help explain these and other Social Security maximizing strategies. Please take the time to understand all the different strategies for taking Social Security benefits. If you have any questions concerning Social Security call 1-800-772-1213.

B. MEDICARE

Medicare will become your primary health insurance when you reach age 65, and your UAL coverage (if you keep it) becomes secondary.

You must sign up for Medicare three months before your 65th birthday to maximize your benefit and minimize your costs. Sign up at the Social Security website, www.socialsecurity.gov. The Medicare website www.medicare.gov is a good source of information regarding Medicare. If you fly until you are 65 years old, you will go right into Medicare. Medicare will cover you on the first day of the month you turn 65. Medicare Part A will be free and Medicare Part B has a premium. UAL will continue to cover you under active medical benefits through the end of your birth month and UAL insurance will be the primary payer of your insurance needs for that month.

For your birth month, even though you have Medicare, UAL insurance will handle your insurance needs. Due to this fact, having Medicare Part A and Part B for that month is extra coverage. Since Medicare Part B has a premium, you should commence Medicare Part B the month after your birth month to save one month of Part B premiums. For example, you turn 65 on March 5th. You will receive active UAL medical until March 31st. If you applied for Medicare Part A and Part B three months prior, your Medicare benefits will commence on March 1st. Since Part B has a premium, it will save you one month of Part B premiums by delaying the start of Part B until April 1st.

There is one exception to this guidance. UAL has taken the stance that a pilot who has his 65th birthday on the first of a month will go into Medicare the day he turns 65. For instance if the pilot's birthday is March 1, after-Medicare will commence on March 1st, not April 1st. ALPA disagrees with this interpretation but until this is resolved it is the pilot's best interest to commence Medicare Part B on his birthday for a pilot who has a birthday on the first day of a month.

C. TRICARE

Some military retirees may have access to medical insurance through TRICARE. The website for RICARE can be found at www.tricare.mil. Military retirees may be able to join the Military Officers Association of America (www.moaa.org) and obtain TRICARE supplemental insurance if desired.

D. HEALTH CARE TAX CREDIT

If you should retire early, and begin PBGC benefit payments prior to age 65, you will receive an eligibility kit from the HCTC program for the Health Care Tax Credit. This credit will not apply to most UAL pilots because you are disqualified for the HCTC if you stay enrolled in the UAL medical insurance or participate in your spouse's employer medical plan (if premiums are taken out pre-tax) or have Tricare. HCTC qualifying health plans include COBRA and individual health plans. Once you turn 65 and enroll in Medicare you are no longer eligible for the HCTC. Visit the HCTC site (link above) to learn more.

3. RETIREMENT COUNTDOWN CHECKLIST

1 Year Before Retirement:

Familiarize yourself with Social Security, Medicare, PBGC, and the myriad of options available to you with each of these programs. Consider contacting professionals (i.e. financial planners or government benefit specialists) to help you make important future decisions. Consider how you are going to obtain medical insurance and how much it is going to cost.

This is the ideal time to start transitioning to your retirement budget.

EWM Clients: Start transitioning to Advanced Cash Management™.

3-4 Months Before Retirement:

- Minimum amount of lead time you want to give Social Security, Medicare, and the PBGC.
- Opt-out of LTD
- EWM Clients: Schedule a disbursement policy interview

1-2 months before retirement:

- Minimum amount of notice you want to give the Company for your retirement letter

- Do you want to order a retirement photo and place it in OPS to be signed?

- Ensure that your future Social Security, PBGC, retirement account distributions, etc. are going to the correct bank account to cover your bills now that your UAL paychecks aren't going there anymore.

- EWM Clients: We'll be setting up Advanced Cash Management™ if not already in place.

- Arrange the details of your retirement flight (ID, arrange BP3 for spouse)

1-2 months after retirement:

- Have you received your final paycheck?

- Do you want to roll over your PRAP balances to a different brokerage? Make sure all of your final deposits from the company have been made before the rollover. EWM Clients: We will delay rollovers until it's confirmed that no future deposits will occur.

- Select your UAL medical benefits, COBRA, etc., if desired. Remember, the Company only pays for medical for two months and you don't want coverage to lapse. If you opt not to choose a UAL medical plan, remember to suspend your coverage so you have the option to return to the UAL medical plan in the future. If you waive coverage you may not be able to return to UAL medical.

4. CHAPTER 3 APPENDIX ITEMS

Four types of benefits

Broadly speaking, your benefits fall into one of four categories:

Cat. I: Classic Pensions, formally known as Defined Benefit (DB) plans or the "A-Plan"

Cat. II: Defined Contribution plans, recognized as the 401(k), the "B-Plan" and "C-Plan" (legacy UAL only), and the "SERP" (Supplemental Employee Retirement Plan) for senior management pilots.

Cat. III: New hybrid insurance savings plans, such as the VEBA RHA, the HSA, FSA, and the MetLife VUL insurance products

Cat. IV: More traditional benefits along with attractive new retiree medical benefits for the pilots.

CAT. II: Defined Contribution Plans

A closer look at the PRAP

The new PRAP will permit employee contributions up to the limits established by Section 415(c) of the Internal Revenue Code. There will be a 16 percent direct employer contribution and 100 percent immediate vesting (and immediate participation) from the pilot's date of hire. The PRAP will continue the new Roth 401k option, which makes sense for younger first officers who have not yet moved out of the lower marginal tax rates.

Direct employer contributions that cannot be contributed due to the limits under sections 401(a)(17) or 415(c) of the Internal Revenue Code shall be forfeited. Instead, an equivalent amount shall be contributed to the RHA VEBA (more information on the RHA VEBA appears in the next section).

No UAL stock will be permitted in the 401k (except as bought by the individual in the brokerage window).

There will be a brokerage window with Schwab. A great feature that's available through Schwab is the "Guided Choice" product. Schwab offers an automated asset allocation feature that's established using the results of a risk tolerance questionnaire completed online. Many pilots will be well served by this excellent and free service.

Supplemental Employee Retirement Plan (SERP)

Worthy of just a brief mention is the SERP plan offered to a very small number of senior management pilots. The line pilot won't be affected by this, and may not even know it exists.

This is a 'top hat' plan that was implemented for management pilots to replace lost A-Plan benefits accrued during periods when they were not eligible as line-pilots. It actually loses value from 60 to 65 because it provided 'unreduced benefits for pilots 60 – 65'. This benefit cannot be taken as an annuity and is 'grossed-up' to pay the taxes incurred as a result of the forced distribution of the lump sum as taxable income.

Important to understand is that, to maintain deferred income status, this plan is "at risk." In case of a bankruptcy, the assets of the SERP would be subject to the demands of the creditors and almost certainly wiped out.

This benefit was effectively frozen when the A-Plan freeze was implemented and will disappear over time as the beneficiaries retire.

CAT. III: Hybrid Insurance Savings Plans

The RHA VEBA

We've prepared detailed scenarios for our clients describing how you can manipulate your RHA VEBA contributions if your income is between $210,000 and $260,000. These scenarios are beyond the scope of this book, but we discuss them with clients at least annually.

There are a couple of important rules to remember: You can't contribute after-tax dollars to a VEBA. Also, vacation forfeitures roll into the VEBA only if the 415(c) limit has already been met. When can you access these funds? Only upon retirement or separation from the airline.

Who is an eligible dependent? Your spouse, disabled children and able-bodied children age 26 or younger. Right now the Defense of Marriage Act is a bit of an issue. It hasn't been established whether a nontraditional couple can submit claims.

Health Savings Accounts

Inheriting an HSA

If the account holder designated his or her spouse as the designated beneficiary, the surviving spouse shall be treated as the account holder of the HSA after the account holder's death. This means that when the account holder dies, if the surviving spouse is the designated beneficiary, then the surviving spouse assumes the account automatically. If a non-spouse beneficiary (other than the estate) is the designated beneficiary, then the HSA ceases to be an HSA on the date of death, and the fair market value of the account on the date of death is treated as taxable to a non-spouse beneficiary for said taxable year.

CAT. IV: Retiree Medical Benefits and Traditional Insurance Options

Retiree Medical Benefits

Before-Medicare Medical Benefits: Except for any HMO, the required contribution for each month of coverage under a particular before-Medicare coverage option and coverage tier elected is equal to a percentage of the total projected cost of that coverage option and coverage tier, based on the pilot's years of service, as follows:

Years of Service	Percentage of Cost
Fewer than 20	80%
20 to 25	60%
25 and over	40%

Retiree medical benefits available to the deceased pilot's survivors and dependents

This only applies to the surviving eligible dependents of eligible deceased pilots, concerning their entitlement to retiree medical benefits.

- *Survivors of Pilots Who Die Before Retirement:* The survivor's medical coverage shall continue to be provided to each surviving eligible dependent until retiree medical benefit coverage is offered.

- *Enrollment of Surviving Eligible Dependents in Retiree Medical Benefit Coverage:* When retiree medical benefit coverage is offered, all eligible dependents of the deceased pilot shall be given the opportunity to enroll in such coverage. The Medicare-eligible dependents may enroll for After-Medicare Medical Benefits and are responsible for paying the required monthly contributions.

- *Medical Coverage of Surviving Eligible Dependents of Pilots Who Die While Retired:* The surviving eligible dependents of a pilot who dies while retired shall continue to be eligible for retiree medical benefits on the same basis as if the pilot had not died. Required monthly contributions must be paid by the surviving eligible dependents.

- If a surviving eligible dependent is eligible for Medicare, then Medicare shall be the primary payer, to the extent permitted by law, and the coverage option elected shall be the secondary payer. As the secondary payer, the coverage option elected shall coordinate benefits with Medicare Part A (hospital insurance) and Medicare Part B (medical insurance) whether or not the individual is enrolled in Medicare.

- Pilots shall be entitled to survivor retiree medical coverage provisions that are no less favorable than the medical coverage provisions for any other employee group— other than provisions limited in their application to corporate offices, executive vice-presidents and above.

Are there any guarantees? A word about Guaranteed Minimum Withdrawal Benefit (GMWB) Variable Annuities

We briefly discussed these in the body of the book.

As stated in the book, let's follow the money: In insurance, a variable annuity with a guaranteed minimum withdrawal benefit is supposed to give you market upside with a guarantee for the return of principal over a 7 to 10 year window. But how good is that guarantee? The product is popular with commission sales people, and they get paid well. For a $1 million policy, they're looking at perhaps $50,000 in commission. That's probably enough to justify feeding 20 people for dinner. If you're a salesperson who sells two of these products—that's a $100,000 paycheck for one night's work. Not bad.

Just remember that, in the end, you're paying for these distribution costs out of future returns.

For this type of product to be legal, it must be built within in an insurance "wrapper." That insurance wrapper allows for a tax deferral on income. I've always believed that it should be illegal to put an IRA into an insurance wrapper because you already have a tax deferral. Why pay twice?

In addition to the product's insurance charge are the underlying funds which tend to charge expense ratios of approximately 1.5 percent to 2.5 percent. So we're looking at an aggregate cost structure in the range of 3.5 percent to 5 percent a year for a lot of these products. That's why insurance companies love these products.

So what? If the insurer can give you what they promised, then why not use these products?

Because the "promise" isn't really worth anything. In almost all 7-to-10 year periods in market history, if one follows a disciplined asset allocation and rebalancing strategy, the expected portfolio recovery window becomes anywhere from three to five years to break even from a severe bear market. So, the promise of "return of principal over the next 10 years" is like me saying, "Well, let me tell you how this works. The only way we're not going to give you your money back is if things get *so bad* that we have a history-making loss from which we cannot recover over a 10 year window."

There's one risk that can't be avoided with a well-designed portfolio "—unsystematic risk." Unsystematic risk is the risk of being entirely invested in just one company. "Wait a minute," you say. "The insurance product is diversified." Really? Your unsystematic risk in a guaranteed annuity product is that the insurer (that sold the product to you) will fail. If the insurer fails, you'll still get your 40 percent or 50 percent after that market disaster, but the insurer's guarantee becomes worthless.

Some may say, "Well, that can't happen." But it *did* happen not too long ago. Several insurers failed in 2007. Because the severity of the market crash was so great then, and because the big insurer was AIG, the government bailed AIG out. But, you are relying on a bailout. If your insurer is a smaller company, or if other situations exist, or if the public has "bailout fatigue," then no one can guarantee what will happen to your policy.

GMWB variable annuities are right for certain people. However, usually the scenarios for which these annuities are beneficial are rare, and they often involve extraordinary liability exposure or other unusual situations. We have yet to recommend this type of product to a client.

A guarantee that works better than an annuity with a GMWB

Are there any guarantees? As we discussed previously, using the "retire-and-suspend" strategy with your A-Plan, you can now count on a larger annuity in retirement from CPRP.

Defer Social Security to age 70 and let it grow at about 8 percent. File and suspend your defined benefit plan, and let it grow at 8 to 10 percent.

Your combined, government-underwritten benefit (pension and Social Security) at age 70 will likely cover all or most of your retirement needs. Also, the Social Security portion will be inflation adjusted.

So how do you fund from retirement at age 65 to 70?

During this important period in your life, you should take the funds you'll need and build a four-year TIPS ladder. Don't buy a TIPS mutual fund. Don't buy a TIPS exchange-rated fund. You take 80 percent of what you'll need to live on for five years and split it among the four TIPS. Set aside 20 percent for your first year's expenses.

You now have four TIPS that you've bought directly from the Treasury. You can get them through Schwab and there's only a slight bid-ask spread involved. Or, you can go to the Treasury directly and buy a one-year TIP, a two-year TIP, a three-year TIP, and a four-year TIP.

Each of those TIPS will mature in each of the next four years prior to your reaching age 70. At age 70, you will have enjoyed an inflation adjusted income that has not been depreciated, regardless of what the inflation rate has been. You can now kick into your deferred Social Security/CPRP annuity program which has a 100 percent probability of matching your longevity.

Any remaining assets, after pre-funding the first five years (including the TIPS purchases), should be placed in an equity-oriented asset allocation. This is how you duplicate the upside guarantee that the GMWB promises—at a far lower cost and with no principal risk.

Is there a downside? Again, with limited retirement resources, you may not be able to execute this strategy. Also, there are hybrid variations that may permit a larger estate for your heirs. We can talk you through these options if you wish.

An alternative strategy that more closely resembles the GMWB promise with absolutely zero end-risk is to purchase what's known as zero coupon bonds with a maturity value of the total investment (say, $1 million at today's discounted value, which would be about $850,000 at current low interest rates). The bonds would mature in 7 to 10 years, just like the GMWB promised. Then purchase a low-cost total market equity index with the remaining funds ($150,000). You are guaranteed a return of principal at the end of the period (due to the maturing zero coupon treasury bonds) and all the market appreciation of the equity index. Zero risk with an upside and no sales fees.

4. RESOURCES

Schwab Retirement Plan Center

If you're using the PRAP, the website for direct to the Schwab Retirement Plan center can be found at PRAP Schwab 1-866-687-7327

www.schwabplan.com/PRAP

United Airlines

Employee Service Center: 1-877-UAL-ESC9

UAL Benefits Center
M-F 7am – 7pm CT
1-800-651-1007

https://flyingtogether.ual.com/
Flying Together >Employee Services > Benefits > Your Benefits Resources

Hewitt has retirement annuity and lump sum information, your Retiree Health Account (RHA), health and insurance information available.

Skynet Retirement and Money Matters
https://flyingtogether.ual.com/active/content.jsp?SID=EmplSvcs&path=/links/CompBen_Retirmt-MoneyMatters.jsp

Useful phone numbers
https://flyingtogether.ual.com/
Flying Together > Employee Services > Benefits Contacts

PBGC 1-800-400-7242 www.pbgc.gov
Social Security 1-800-772-1213 www.socialsecurity.gov
Medicare 1-800-633-4227 www.medicare.gov
Retired Military Tricare 1-877-874-2273 (this number varies by region, visit website for complete contact information)
www.tricare.mil

Airline Pilot's Association – UAL

The following link provides a plethora of valuable information, including webinars for pilots approaching retirement. If using Internet Explorer, it is recommended you select Compatibility Mode for best viewing.

http://ual.alpa.org/Committees/CommitteesNZ/RetirementInsurance/tabid/3670/Default.aspx

UAL ALPA Retirement Seminars

The following seminars are as good as it gets for educating yourself in a video format about the various benefits discussed in Chapter 3.

Retirement Seminar 1: Intro/Vacation Bidding in Final Year/Retirement Administration Items

http://vimeo.com/user13985327/review/69318491/ace7380dea

Retirement Seminar 2: Retiree Medical Benefits and Medicare

http://vimeo.com/user13985327/review/69169745/6fba41f812

Retirement Seminar 3: Retiree Health Accounts (RHA) and PRAP Distributions at Retirement

http://vimeo.com/user13985327/review/69171920/f2e6729f4b

Retirement Seminar 4: Retiree PBGC Benefits
http://vimeo.com/user13985327/review/69174865/972277460b

Retirement Seminar 5: Social Security Benefits, Annuities and Financial Advisors
An important seminar on social security benefits, equity indexed annuities and researching financial advisors. Discusses understanding advisor motivations for various recommendations. If you watch only one of these videos, watch this one.

http://vimeo.com/user13985327/review/69176944/856ea1c1ed

5. FINANCIAL PLANNING ORGANIZATIONS

Financial Planning Association® (FPA®)

The Financial Planning Association® (FPA®) is the largest membership organization for CFP® professionals in the U.S. and also includes members who support the financial planning process. Working in alliance with academic leaders, legislative and regulatory bodies, financial services firms and consumer interest organizations, FPA® helps connect all in our membership through a variety of unique and compelling ways.

FPA® members adhere to the highest standards of professional competence, ethical conduct and clear, complete disclosure to those they serve. FPA® membership consists of Certified Financial Planners,™ educators, financial services professionals, students and more; FPA® is compensation neutral and represents those from diverse backgrounds and business models. FPA®'s unique network of nationwide chapters encourages professional development and networking on a local level.

http://www.fpanet.org/

National Association of Professional Financial Advisors (NAPFA)

The National Association of Personal Financial Advisors (NAPFA) is the country's leading professional association of fee-only financial advisors—highly trained professionals who are committed to working in the best interests of those they serve. Since 1983, Americans across the country have looked to NAPFA for access to financial professionals who meet the highest membership standards for professional competency, client-focused financial planning, and fee-only compensation.

http://www.napfa.org/

Efficient Wealth Management LLC

Efficient Wealth Management is a fiduciary, fee-only registered investment advisory (RIA) firm, located in The Woodlands, Texas, dedicated to providing for the needs of United Airlines' pilots and executives. All of our Wealth Managers are degreed CFP® professionals.

www.EfficientWealthManagement.com

ABOUT
PAUL CARROLL

Paul J. Carroll, CFP,® is the principal and founder of Efficient Wealth Management, which provides consultative wealth management solutions to airline professionals and other high-net-worth individuals in the Houston, Texas area. Working with his team of experts, Paul helps affluent clients address their biggest financial concerns: preserving their wealth; mitigating taxes; taking care of their heirs; ensuring their assets aren't unjustly taken; and charitable giving.

Paul uses a consultative process to gain a detailed understanding of his clients' deepest values and goals. He then employs customized recommendations designed to address each client's unique needs and goals.

Successful airline pilots and other clients work with Paul to:

- Develop and implement a comprehensive wealth management plan to help them reach their financial dreams.

- Make smarter decisions in today's uncertain political, economic and social environment.

- Obtain an independent second opinion from a top financial advisor in their community.

Paul is uniquely positioned to understand the needs of the professional airline pilot. He is a licensed pilot, type-rated in a number of Boeing and Airbus jets, and has served as a captain at United (Continental) Airlines. He is a Certified Financial Planner™ with a Master's degree in Finance from Texas A&M University. Previously, Paul was a financial advisor with Smith Barney.

Paul is active in the local chapter of the Financial Planning Association and was awarded Houston's Top Wealth Managers Award for 2013 by the Houston Business Journal. He has authored a number of articles, white papers and video presentations addressing various financial advanced planning issues. These are available in the "Who We Are" section of our website www.EfficientWealthManagement.com.

ABOUT EFFICIENT WEALTH MANAGEMENT

Efficient Wealth Management is a boutique wealth management practice founded in 2005 that offers personal, private and exclusive concierge-level service for successful airline pilots. We are a fee-only firm, never accepting commissions or other transaction-oriented compensation. We limit our focus to select clients for whom we believe we can have a tremendous impact.

Using a consultative process, we work in conjunction with a team of experts to help our clients build and preserve their wealth, plan for retirement, mitigate their income taxes, take care of their heirs, and protect their assets.

The Efficient Wealth Management team has a unique understanding of pilots' needs. Our experts are intimately familiar with the new United's pension plans and the Pension Protection Act of 2006. We are well suited to help pilots dealing with the uncertainties of the airline industry and the Continental/United merger.

If you feel that our wealth management process might be a fit for you, please contact us at 281-528-1200. We will set up a discovery meeting to explore whether we should work together. If we find that we are not the right firm for you, we will do our best to refer you to a more appropriate advisor.

To learn more, please visit our website at www.EfficientWealthManagement.com.